Essays on
Individuality

A Liberty*Press* Edition

Essays on Individuality

Edited and with an Introduction
by Felix Morley

Foreword to the Second Edition
by Arthur Kemp

Liberty Fund

Indianapolis
1977

Liberty*Press* is a publishing imprint of Liberty Fund, Inc., a foundation established to encourage study of the ideal of a society of free and responsible individuals.

The cuneiform inscription that serves as the design motif for our endpapers is the earliest-known written appearance of the word "freedom" *(ama-gi),* or "liberty." It is taken from a clay document written about 2300 B.C. in the Sumerian city-state of Lagash.

Library of Congress Cataloging in Publication Data

Morley, Felix, 1894–1982
  Essays on individuality.

  Includes indexes.
  1. Individualism. 2. Individuality. I. Title.
HM136.M814 1977   301.11´3   76–30745
ISBN 0-913966-28-2

10 9 8 7 6 5 4 3

Contents

Foreword to the Second Edition

Only a few months longer than two decades ago, the twelve authors of these essays gathered at the Princeton Inn to criticize, discuss and comment upon their individual contributions. From an historical perspective, two decades are little more than an instant in time; but from the viewpoint of an individual person—and individuality and personality comprised the basic subject matter of these essays—two decades are a substantial proportion of the Biblical allotment of three score years and ten. To me, as director and organizer of that Symposium, and doubtless also to Felix Morley as its beneficent chairman as well as participant, twenty years is a very long time.

But, long as it is, I remember it well, and for several reasons. As an economist, it was the first time I had organized a multi-disciplinary conference involving scholars whose specialties were in the humanities, the physical sciences, the social sciences, history and politics as well as economics. The resulting discussions, probably inevitably, melded into philosophy. This was reinforced by the fortunate, perhaps fortuitous, selection of a group of men who had both the courage and the intellectual capacity to transcend the limits of their respective specialties in order to consider the problems of society as a whole, particularly those relating to individual privacy, individual responsibility, and individual freedom of thought and action.

Readers of these essays will not be able fully to appreciate the value of open, uninhibited discussion which results from participants speaking directly *to* each other, instead of *through* each other to an audience. Yet this contributed greatly to the quality of the resulting book when it was first published as well as now, when the problems discussed in these essays are as important as, if not more important than, they were two decades ago.

One discussion, still vivid in my memory, began with unanimous agreement that there existed no *science* of ethics as such. This led to the deeper question of whether or not a science of ethics could develop or be developed—a question which Professor Zirkle, not without hesitation, undertook to answer affirmatively based upon his particular specialty, genetics. Ethics, as a science, he proposed, might develop out of the principle that what is good is that which protects, preserves and promotes the survival and expansion of the species; in short, the ethical principle of women and children first. Unfortunately there is no way of reproducing here the flood of objections raised by the other participants. I do recall very well Professor Hayek's quiet assertion that such a proposition not only presupposed knowledge of what did, in fact, preserve and protect the species, but also presupposed that it was a single cause and not a choice among, or interaction between, several causes. "Is it," he asked, "more ethical if the population were to double in thirty years rather than in sixty—or would it be the reverse?"

The interesting thing in retrospect is not so much the ensuing discussion, excellent as it was, as what was not said. As far as I am able to recollect, there was no discussion of some related ethical questions which surely would be raised today. These have to do with the distinct probability that science is able, or within the next two decades will be able, to introduce conscious, guided genetic selection into the so-called natural selection process of human beings. Like it or not, some interdisciplinary group in the not too distant future will have to raise some very difficult ethical questions. I hope the surviving members of the 1956 Princeton Symposium can be persuaded to participate in the discussions. The others doubtless will have reserved superior positions of audibility and observation.

The year 1976 called forth frequent references to Adam Smith, the "father of economics" (a dubious phrase, since he was a life-long bachelor). Those of us responsible for the 1956 Symposium should give thanks for the efficacy of Smith's "invisible hand" in selecting two economists, both of whom some twenty years later would have received Nobel laureates in economics: Friedrich A. Hayek and Milton Friedman. Whether this was due to remarkable foresight and perspicacity on our part or to the fortuitious operation of the "invisible hand," today's readers must decide for themselves. Either way, the essays written by these men still speak eloquently and with remarkable clarity.

It might be said of these essays, as it can be said of the years between 1956 and 1976, that some were better than others. Taken as a whole, however, these essays hold up very well indeed, and like fine Cabernet Sauvignon, some have greatly improved and mellowed with age. Let us hope that today's readers will conclude, so far as essays on individuality are concerned, that 1956 was a very good year.

ARTHUR KEMP

Claremont Men's College
Claremont, California
November 3, 1976

Introduction

The twelve essays composing this volume were originally prepared for a "Symposium on Individuality and Personality" held at the Princeton Inn, Princeton, New Jersey, September 12 to 18, 1956. Most of them have been somewhat revised by the authors, in the light of the symposium discussions, and are now submitted to public consideration as a comprehensive survey of this vital and timely subject.

This symposium was sponsored by the Foundation for American Studies, which in a preliminary announcement noted that since the close of World War II "an increasing number of scholars have turned their attention to the problem of man's freedom in the face of modern society's seemingly irresistible urge to socialize and regiment the thought and action of the individual." It was to give close analysis to the far-reaching implications of this trend that the Foundation gathered together, for free and untrammeled discussion, a group of men "whose writings have shown a particular awareness of the . . . challenge to . . . individual privacy, responsibility, and self-determination. . . ."

The only instruction given to those whose contributions follow was that each should "approach the topic of the symposium from the vantage point of his own specialty." Since the participants had been intentionally selected from various professional fields, uniformity of approach was neither desired, expected nor attained. In the group were specialists in two branches of natural science, in economics, history, literature, philosophy, politics, rhetoric, and sociology. Yet, as the reader will see for himself, the area of fundamental agreement proved itself much more extensive, and much more positive, than the occasional differences of opinion, sharp though these sometimes were.

None of the essays printed in this volume were read at the symposium. They nevertheless clearly reveal not only the scope but also the high degree of interlocking support and intellectual integration in the proceedings. The various papers had been prepared for advance distribution among the participants, each of whom introduced his subject briefly to the group, whose members then engaged in lengthy and lively round-table discussion. Notes on the points debated were kept, then read, amended, and approved at the close of each session.

Finally, these notes were amalgamated into a general summary report of the entire proceedings, prepared by Professor Arthur Kemp of Claremont Men's College, who was Director of the Symposium and in that capacity responsible for its excellent arrangements. The writer in this Introduction served as chairman and was chosen as coordinating editor of this resultant volume. Professor Helmut Schoeck voluntarily contributed both time and talent to compilation of the Index.*

During the sessions there were no guests, no reporters, and indeed no interruptions of any moment. Three daily sessions, held morning, afternoon, and night for four days, absorbed practically all but bedtime for the conferees. Even at meals, in shifting combinations, the participants continued a line of discussion which was of such absorbing interest to all that this present wider distribution of results seems wholly desirable. Few of the members of the symposium had personally known many of the others before this gathering, and one sign of its notable success is the number of continuing friendships founded on the exchanges at the Princeton Inn.

So is it always on an exploration or a pilgrimage. And exploring pilgrims the members of this symposium assuredly were—even though perforce more sedentary than those immortalized by Chaucer. More than one of the group found a certain parallelism with the Canterbury Pilgrims, with the Tabard Inn at Southwark where they assembled, with the rich variety and deep human insight of each and every strongly individualized tale.

There is perhaps another similarity, since in both

---

* A new, enlarged Index has been provided in this second edition—Publisher.

cases the order of presentation has no relationship with intrinsic merit. Indeed, as in the *Canterbury Tales,* each of the following essays owes strength to its federation with other essentially independent units.

But since the beautiful essay of John Dos Passos takes Chaucer as the "fountainhead" of individuality in English literature, to that participant appropriately falls the lead position of that master's "ful worthy" knight. "And he bigan with right a mery chere his tale anon, and seyde in this manere. . . ."

FELIX MORLEY

Gibson Island, Maryland
January 12, 1958

Essays on
Individuality

Essay One

A Question
of Elbow Room

John Dos Passos

Individuality is freedom lived. When we use the word individuality we refer to a whole gamut of meanings. Starting from the meanings which pertain to the deepest recesses of private consciousness, these different meanings can be counted off one by one like the skins in the cross section of an onion, until we reach the everyday outer hide of meaning which crops up in common talk.

When we speak commonly, without exaggerated precision, of an individual, don't we mean a person who has grown up in an environment sufficiently free from outside pressures and restraints to develop his own private evaluations of men and events? He has been able to make himself enough elbow room in society to exhibit unashamed the little eccentricities and oddities that differentiate one man from another man. From within his separate hide he can look out at the world with that certain aloofness which we call dignity. No two men are alike any more than two snowflakes are alike. However a man develops, under conditions of freedom or conditions of servitude, he will still differ from other men. The man in jail will be different from his cellmates but his differences will tend to develop in frustration and hatred. Freedom to develop individuality is inseparable from the attainment of what all the traditions of the race have taught us to consider to be the true human stature.

Fifty years ago all this would have been the rankest platitude, but we live in an epoch where the official directors of opinion through the schools, pulpits, and presses have leaned so far over backwards in their efforts to conform to what they fancy are the exigencies of a society based on industrial mass production, that the defense of individuality has become a life and death matter.

It is a defense that a man takes on at his peril. The very word has become suspect. Even to mention individualism or individuality in circles dedicated to the fashionable ideas of the moment is to expose oneself to ridicule. "Listening to papers on individualism— how boring!" exclaimed a lady to whom I tried to explain over the phone what I was doing in Princeton.

Casting around for examples which might clarify some of the meanings of the word individuality, without seeming too boring, even to heads full of the fashionable negations of the moment, I find myself falling back on English literature as we find it on the library shelves.

I'm thinking of the magnificent series of imaginative writings in modern English that began with Chaucer five hundred years ago. You can make a very good case for the notion that there runs through it all a unifying thread which is the measure of its difference from other literatures. This English literature is dedicated to the description of man not only as an individual but as an eccentric. Naturally it is colored throughout by the peculiar eminence the traditions of English law and of English thought generally gave to individual rights and individual responsibility, but it is flavored, to boot, by a real enjoyment of idiosyncrasy. Perhaps English literature will continue to be the conduit through which our now so discredited passion for personal liberty will be freshened and stimulated by impulses from past generations. The belief in the uniqueness of each human being is, after all, not of yesterday. To the Athenians this belief was incarnate on earth. Primitive Christianity turned it inside out and established it in heaven. Our practical English forebears managed to bring it down to earth again.

Their earthy individuality is the heart of our literary inheritance. To root that inheritance out of our minds you'll have to pull the English classics off the shelves of our libraries. The American educational process, with its bias towards conformity on the basis of the lowest common denominator, has not managed to do quite that, at least not yet; but it has succeeded in letting the classical literature molder in innocuous desuetude in the dust of the unvisited stacks. Scrape the mildew off the backs of the books and you'll find them as ready as ever to fill the imagination with a rich spawn of cantankerous human beings.

Chaucer is the fountainhead. Right at the beginning, in the earliest days of the formation of the language, you'll find in the *Canterbury Tales* the characteristics which are to be the special earmark of English literature for the next five hundred years. The minute you step into that Tabard Inn at Southwark, in the first few lines of the prologue, you find yourself part of the pilgrimage of all the great characters of English storytelling. Right away the poet starts describing people, individuals he enjoys for their own sake. Already he shows the down-to-earth knowledge of vulgar reality, the gift for jocose narrative, the appetite for freedom and elbow room, the sharp satire mellowed by fellow feeling for a great many varieties of men. These are the qualities which are to characterize the whole literature to come. You feel behind every word and phrase the driving force of Chaucer's enthusiasm for individuality in his fellow man, even indeed for eccentricity and oddity.

Not only the men but the women are individuals. It is in Chaucer that there first appears a certain special attitude towards women. The women have as much private and personal individuality as the men. Compare them with the women in the French romances of the period. In the prologue to the *Canterbury Tales,* and in the marvelous interludes between, you meet real women, humorously and tenderly and understandingly described, women who stand up in their own right and say their own say in the world. The Prioress and the Wife of Bath are the first of a long line of large-scale portraits of women; the women of Shakespeare's plays from Mistress Quickly and Juliet's nurse to Hamlet's mother and Lady Macbeth; the hapless solitary figure of Vittoria Corombona in the Duchess of Malfi, the pert matrons of Restoration comedy, the aware young ladies walking on the lawns of Jane Austen's country houses, Dickens' female gargoyles out of the London slums, and the inimitable Becky Sharpe.

Chaucer's men are a zestful crew. They have the high spirits of people with plenty of elbow room in the world. The foulmouthed innkeeper, the scoundrelly pardoner, the miller and the reeve, the cynical merchant, the wealthy franklin in whose house it snowed of meat and drink, who foreshadowed Squire Western and Mr. Wardle the genial landlord of Dingly Dell, the lawyer who was such a very busy man and yet seemed ever busier than he was, the mildspoken knight and his well-bred son, the squire who left half told the story of Cambuscan bold.

And through it all the feeling of the road. A man is never more his single separate self than when he sets out on a journey. A man is on his own on the road. This excitement of adventuring from place to place will reappear in some of Defoe's narratives and in Tom Jones' burlesque adventures and in the tribulations of Smollett's rascally heroes and in the preposterous travels of the Pickwickians and the contemplative excursions of Thoreau and George Borrow.

From the *Canterbury Tales* on there is insight to be gained by thinking of the mainstream of the literature as a continuation of Chaucer's pilgrimage. With the coming of the English Renaissance there appear, to be sure, the towering figures of leaders of men painted with breathless haste on the huge canvasses of Marlowe and Shakespeare; individuality on a superhuman scale facing the dilemmas, the crimes, the failures, the glories of the untrammeled will.

The comically sketched low-lives are pushed into the shadow. But even in Shakespeare's plays the Chaucerian preoccupation with the laughable idiosyncrasies of all sorts of men has gone on developing as a contrasting background to the romantic passions and the bombast of the tragic roles that fill the center of the stage. This background is often on the edge of becoming the foreground. Though Sir John Falstaff seems to have been invented as a mere foil for Prince Hal, he soon developed, in response to the audience's demands, as a protagonist in his own right. The fat knight and his rowdy crew would have found themselves thor-

oughly at home among the Canterbury pilgrims. As
their story evolves through four plays it becomes one
of the precursors of the English novel.

While the gaudy romanticism of the age of Elizabeth
tears itself to tatters, the Chaucerian sort of comic naturalism subsists in the dramatists who are trying to
reproduce the classical comedy of manners. With the
reopening of the theaters the comedy of idiosyncrasy
will dominate the stage. With the emergence of prose
narrative in Swift's satires and in Defoe's common-
sensical tales the depiction of individuals will become
the main business of the writer. As the modern novel
is born out of Fielding's gargantuan amusement at
Richardson's attempt to turn the art of fictional narrative into an apology for the ideas and prejudices of
the rising shopkeeper class, the Chaucerian naturalism
and the Chaucerian satire become its very substance.

With *Tom Jones* the novel is established as the
chronicle of individuality. By the time Sterne writes
his *Tristram Shandy* the theme is so thoroughly established that he can treat his reader to endless whimsical
variations. In the nineteenth century, when novel-
writing will become the passion of the age, Sterne's
whimsies will reappear in more Chaucerian form in
Charles Dickens' portrait gallery of comic characters.
Somehow the English of the great tradition managed,
no matter from what low caste they sprang, to maintain enough elbow room about them to cherish this

appreciation of individuality as the central pleasure of their lives.

It is certainly no accident that the political institutions which grew up in the society that produced this literature of individualism should have been individualistic too. When all the discussions of the position of man in the framework of government that had obsessed so many of the best minds of the century came to a focus in 1776, the chief preoccupation of the state builders in America was to establish institutions in their new country which would allow each citizen enough elbow room to grow into individuality. They differed greatly on how best to bring about that state of affairs but there was no disagreement on fundamental aims. Protection of the individual's happiness—the assurance of the elbow room he needed to reach his full stature— was the reason for the state's existence.

Thomas Jefferson and Gouverneur Morris held very differing views on the problems of government. Jefferson was an agrarian democrat who believed that every man was capable of taking some part in the government of the community; Morris was a city-bred aristocrat who believed that only men to whom wealth and position had given the advantage of a special education were capable of dealing with public affairs; but when Morris wrote George Washington his definition of statesmanship—"I mean politics in the great Sense, or that sublime Science which embraces for its Object the

Happiness of Mankind"—he meant the same thing by
the word happiness as Jefferson did when he wrote it
into the Declaration of Independence. To both men it
meant elbow room. Elbow room is positive freedom.

Consult any sociologist today as to the meaning of
happiness in the social context and he'll be pretty sure
to tell you it means adjustment. Adjustment, if it is
freedom at all, is freedom of a very negative sort. It
certainly is the opposite of elbow room.

To both Morris and Jefferson the "sublime Science"
consisted of designing a government that would allow
the greatest possible freedom to its citizens; to the
political leaders and theorizers of today the "sublime
Science" consists in teaching the citizen to adjust
himself to the demands of society and state. He has to
learn to put up with an ever-increasing lack of elbow
room.

We are hardly conscious of the immensity of the
change which has taken place in the aims of state
building because we still use the vocabulary of our individualist tradition in literature and politics. The
change has been so gradual through the years that we
have failed to notice that the words don't apply any
more to the facts they are supposed to describe. This
lag in definition makes it extremely difficult to project
our traditional notions of individuality, which are still
thoroughly cogent in their own context, into the mid-
twentieth-century society we have to live in. Perhaps
the reason why we are so uncomfortable with the very

term "individuality" is that its redefinition will bring us up against a set of realities highly unpleasant to face.

It's startling to remember that only a hundred and thirty years, merely the span of a couple of lifetimes, have gone by since Jefferson died at Monticello, on the same Independence Day of 1826 when his old friend and political opponent, John Adams, died at Braintree near Boston, whispering, so the old tradition has it: "Thomas Jefferson still survives."

These years have seen such a transformation in the shape of American society that the age of Jefferson and Adams and Washington and Madison and Hamilton and the rest seems as far away as the age of Confucius.

People in late eighteenth-century America tended to live out their lives grouped into one of two kinds of social organization. There was the New England–type town where social standing depended on a combination of godliness with that possession of this world's goods which was the outward expression of divine favor. The tendency toward social stratification in at least the eastern Massachusetts towns was well expressed by the fact that at Harvard College students were listed according to their social standing instead of according to their scholastic ability. That doesn't mean that literacy wasn't highly regarded. The New Englanders were people of the book. Nor does it mean that they were not politically democratic. Their government was the town meeting where every man had his say. The society which produced the Adamses was a democracy tempered by aristocracy.

To the southward there was the plantation society, which produced George Mason and Jefferson. There men were rated according to the acreage of their lands. In the Virginia county governments, as in rural England, the landowners were the law. Both of these systems were subject to the democratizing influence of the ebb and flow of the continually renewed pioneer enterprises of the new settlements, where skill and courage and the push necessary for survival were the most admired qualities, and where universal manhood suffrage was the political rule. The men of energy and initiative tended to be attracted to the frontier. The educated men, the men of book learning, of all these differing communities were steeped in that spirit of *noblesse oblige* which had been the noble obverse of the arrogance and self-seeking of the British ruling gentry.

The thing all the Americans—townsmen, fishermen, and sailors of the New England seaports; planters and merchants from round the Chesapeake; hunters and furtraders from the Ohio—had in common was that they thoroughly understood the world they lived in. The technology was simple. From the age of the Hebrew prophets to the time of the American revolution the basic operations by which men sowed crops for food and produced clothing and shelter had changed remarkably little. Since the renaissance period there had been a great improvement in tools, but production was still based on the skill of the hand and the arm and the eye. Manufacture meant making by hand.

The family was still almost everywhere the central productive unit, as it was the central social unit. Manufacture, trade, farming, and the professions were conducted on a family basis. The work of apprentices, indentured servants, Negro slaves on the plantations in the South, all meshed into the framework of a man and his wife and their sons and daughters coping with life as a group.

Any tolerably bright individual knew from personal experience how wheeled carriages and sailing ships worked, understood the processes of agriculture and manufacturing, the use of money, and the technique of buying and selling on the marketplace. Much more important, they all knew by direct personal experience how the different kinds of people worked who made up their society.

They took human cussedness for granted.

The outstanding fact you learn from reading the letters of the men of that day was that none of them had any illusions about how men behaved in the political scheme. A radical idealist like Jefferson allowed for the self-interest (real or imagined) of the average voter, or for the vanity and ambition and greed of the officeholder, as much as a cynical conservative like Gouverneur Morris. The difference was that they applied their knowledge according to different theories as to what sort of government would most desirably influence human behavior. Jefferson thought that under proper institutions individuals could be indefinitely improved. Like his Scottish contemporary, Adam Smith, he trusted to the workings of enlightened self-interest.

Both parties understood the common man as well as any of the more desperate demogogues we have with us today. They allowed for his self-seeking, for his shortsightedness, his timidity, his abominable apathy, his only intermittent public spirit. The difference was that the statesmen of the early republic used that "sublime Science" in the service of their great state-building aims. Using men as they found them, they managed to set up the system of balanced self-government which made possible the exuberant growth of the United States.

In Jefferson's day the average citizen had a fair understanding of most of the workings of the society he lived in. The years that stretch between us and the day of his death have seen the shape of industry transformed in rapid succession by steam power, electric power, the internal combustion engine, and, now, by jet propulsion and the incredibly proliferating possibilities of power derived from nuclear fission and fusion. Any social system of necessity molds itself into shapes laid down by the daily occupations of the individual men who form its component parts. The mass-production methods of assembly-line industry have caused a society made up of individuals grouped in families to give way to a society made up of individuals grouped in factories and office buildings, for whom family life has been relegated to the leisure hours.

Life in our drastically changing industrial world has become so cut up into specialized departments and vocabularies, and has become so hard to understand and to see as a whole, that most people won't even try. Even people of first-rate intelligence, at work in various segregated segments of our economy, tend to get so walled up in the particular work they are doing that they never look outside of it. Even if they remember that every man has a duty to give some of his time and some of his energy to the general good, they don't know how to go about it.

Enormously complicated political institutions have grown up in response to the exigencies of the industrial framework. Instead of the farming communities which Jefferson expected to be the foundation of self-government we have a population concentrated in cities and suburbs. Instead of living under the least possible government, most of the American people are living under an accumulation of often conflicting sovereignties.

A man working for General Motors in Detroit, for an example, is subject to the management of his corporation, and to the often arbitrary government of the United Auto Workers. He is subject to the traffic police

on the road on his way to and from work, to the taxes
and regulations of the town where he lives, to the taxes
and regulations of the state of Michigan, and to the
ever-expanding authority of the federal government.
Each of the sovereignties has the power to make itself
extremely disagreeable if he crosses its bureaucratic
will. To hold his end up against this panoply of disciplinary powers, the man has only the precarious right
to hold up his hand in the meeting of his union local,
and the right to put his cross on the ballot in an occasional election, opposite the name of some politician he
has perhaps only heard of in the confusion of electoral
ballyhoo.

Is it surprising that the common man is hard to coax
out of the shell of political apathy he has grown to protect himself from the knowledge of his own helplessness? The first step towards restoring to this man a
sense of citizenship would be to explain his situation
to him in terms which had reference to the observable
facts of his daily life. A fresh political vocabulary is
needed before we can try to reset the individual cogs
so that they mesh into the wheels of government.

None of this means that Thomas Jefferson's or John
Adams' aspirations, to build a state which would afford
the greatest possible amount of elbow room to the
greatest number of its citizens, are obsolete. Their
"sublime Science" was based on an understanding of
factors in human behavior which have not changed
since the beginnings of recorded history. Newton's

basic principle of gravitation has not been superseded. It has been amended and amplified by Einstein's formulae. Newton's still remains one of the explanations through which mathematicians cope with the observable facts of physics. In a somewhat similar way, if men could be found to apply to political problems the sort of first-rate rigorous thinking which we have seen applied to physics in our lifetime, and if the study of the science of state building should thus come into its own again, the great formulations of the generation of 1776 would still be found valid.

If there were to grow up in this country a generation of young men and women who felt that the most important thing in life was to restore elbow room to the people of the United States they would find in the records of the founders of the republic a storehouse of the skills and mental attitudes they would need in their work. They would find that every word which was spoken or written on the art of politics between 1775 and 1801 would take on a new urgency.

By a reapplication of the vocabulary of freedom they might find some formula through which to apply the basic tenets of individualism as directly to our daily lives as Jefferson and his friends applied them to the everyday world they knew. Lord knows for the last twenty years we have done enough talking about democracy in this country. Maybe the reason why the talk doesn't turn into useful action is that the terms don't apply to our lives as we live them.

Jefferson's ideas are particularly cogent to us now because among the leaders of the American revolution he led the radical wing which was in favor of more popular rule rather than less. He was the chief leader of the tendency which led us to universal adult suffrage. In a letter he wrote a few days before his death refusing, on account of the state of his health, an invitation to spend the very Fourth of July which was destined to be his last with a group of admirers in Washington City, he spoke happily of the blessings of self-government and of "the free right to the unbounded exercise of reason and freedom of opinion," and rephrased the basic conviction of his life with characteristic vehemence: "The general spread of the light of science has already laid open to every view the palpable truth that the mass of mankind has not been born with saddles on their backs, nor a favored few booted and spurred ready to ride them legitimately by the grace of God."

It is one of the magnificent ironies of history that the zealots for total bureaucratic rule, whose dogma provides them with boots and spurs to ride the mass of mankind, justify themselves by the same political phraseology which the men of Jefferson's day hoped would make forever impossible the regimentation of the many by the few. Unfortunately, the practice of the demagogic dictatorships abroad is not so far from our own as we would like to think. The redeeming feature of our bureaucratic government is that the machinery still subsists within it by which the popular will can effect its transformation in any conceivable direction. All we need is the wit and the will.

It is always well to remember that the commonest practice of mankind is that a few shall impose authority and the majority shall submit. Watch any bunch of children playing during a school recess. It is the habit of individual liberty which is the exception. The liberties we enjoy today, freedom to express our ideas if we have any, freedom to jump in a car and drive any place we want to on the highway, freedom to choose the trade or profession we want to make our living by, are the survivors of the many liberties won by the struggles and pains of generations of English-speaking people who somehow had resistance to authority in their blood. Their passion for individuality instead of conformity was unique in the world. What the generation of 1776 did was to organize those traditions into a new system.

When the British troops marched out of Yorktown to surrender to Washington's army one of their bands played a tune called "The World Turned Upside Down." In the long run the people of the United States have managed to make the promise of that tune come true. Underdog has come mighty near to becoming topdog. The other side of that medal is that the cult of the lowest common denominator has caused brains, originality of mind, quality of thought to be dangerously disparaged. Conformity has been more prized than individuality. All the same, we can write in the credit column that there has never been a society where so many men and women have shared a fellow feeling for so many other men and women. With every change in economic organization new class lines and stratifications have appeared, but they have hardly outlasted a generation or two. The old saying about three generations from shirtsleeves to shirtsleeves has turned out profoundly true. Compared to the rest of mankind, we have come nearest to producing a classless society. Ask any recent immigrant. Nine times out of ten he will tell you that what struck him first in the United States was that feeling of the world turned upside down. The question today is whether, for all its wide distribution of material goods, this classless society offers the individual enough elbow room to make his life worth living.

Right from the beginning the wise men have said that democracy would end in the destruction of liberty. Washington in his last years, and John Adams and the whole Federalist faction, thought universal suffrage would end in demagoguery and despotism. Their reasoning was the basis of the lamentations of the school of Brooks Adams and Henry Adams at the beginning of this century. Hamilton's "your people is a great beast" was echoed by Justice Holmes in his explosion to Carl Becker: "Goddamn them all, I say." Since the earliest days only a small minority have at any time really believed in the privacy of their own consciences that American democracy would work. A state of mind among the learned and the wellborn was admirably expressed in a letter Macaulay wrote to H. N. Randall when Randall was putting the finishing touches on his biography of Jefferson, in the fifties of the last century.

"You are surprised to learn," Macaulay wrote, "I have not a high opinion of Mr. Jefferson and I am surprised at your surprise. I am certain that I never wrote a line and that I never, in parliament, in conversation or even on the hustings—a place where it is the fashion to court the populace—uttered a word advocating the opinion that the supreme authority in a state ought to be entrusted to the majority of citizens told by the head; in other words, to the poorest and most ignorant part of society. I have long been convinced that institutions purely democratic must, sooner or later, destroy liberty or civilization or both.

"You think that your country enjoys an exemption from these evils. I will frankly own to you that I am of a very different opinion. Your fate I believe to be certain, though it is deferred by a physical cause. As long as you have a boundless extent of fertile and unoccupied land, your laboring population will be far more at ease than the laboring population of the old world; and while that is the case the Jeffersonian policy may continue to exist without causing any fatal calamity." [Macaulay is launching the theory of the last frontier which is now popular among certain historians.]

"But the time will come," Macaulay went on, "when New England will be as thickly populated as Old England. Wages will be as low and will fluctuate as much

with you as with us. You will have your Manchesters
and Birminghams. Hundreds and thousands of artisans
will be sometimes out of work. Then your institutions
will be fairly brought to the test. Distress everywhere
makes the laborer mutinous and discontented and in-
clines him to listen with eagerness to agitators who tell
him that it is a monstrous iniquity that one man should
have millions, while another cannot get a full meal. In
bad years there is plenty of grumbling here and sometimes a little rioting. But it matters little for here the
sufferers are not the rulers. The supreme power is in a
class, numerous indeed but select, in an educated class,
in a class which is and knows itself to be deeply interested in, the security of property, and the maintenance of order." [This is the type of government
Gouverneur Morris and Alexander Hamilton wanted.]
"Accordingly, the malcontents are firmly yet gently restrained. The bad time is got over without robbing the
wealthy to relieve the indigent. The springs of national
prosperity soon begin to flow again; work is plentiful,
wages rise and all is tranquility and cheerfulness.

"I have seen England three or four times pass
through such critical seasons as I have described.
Through such seasons the United States will have to
pass, in the course of the next century, if not of this.
How will you pass through them? I heartily wish you a
good deliverance, but my reason and my wishes are at
war and I cannot help foreboding the worst. It is quite
plain your government will never be able to restrain a

distressed and discontented majority. For with you the majority is the government and the rich, who are always a minority, are absolutely at its mercy. The day will come when, in the State of New York a multitude of people, none of whom has had more than half a breakfast or expects to have more than half a dinner, will choose the legislature. Is it possible to doubt what sort of legislature will be chosen? On one side is a statesman preaching patience, respect for vested rights, a strict observance of public faith. On the other side is a demogogue ranting about tyranny of capitalists and usurers, and asking why anybody should be permitted to drink champagne and to ride in a carriage while thousands of honest people are in want of necessities. Which of the two candidates is likely to be preferred by a working man who hears his children cry for bread?

"I seriously apprehend that you will in some such season of adversity as I have described do things which will prevent prosperity from returning; that you will act like people in a year of scarcity who devour all the seed corn and thus make the next year not one of scarcity but of absolute distress. The distress will produce fresh spoliation. There is nothing to stay you. Your constitution is all sail and no anchor. As I said, when society has entered on this downward progress, either civilization or liberty must perish. Either some Caesar or Napoleon will seize the reins of government with a strong hand or your Republic will be as fearfully plundered and laid waste by barbarians in the twentieth century as the Roman Empire was in the fifth; with this difference, that the Huns and Vandals who ravaged the Roman Empire came from without, and your Huns and Vandals will have been engendered within your own country by your own institutions.

"Thinking this, of course I cannot reckon Jefferson among the benefactors of mankind."

Macaulay's practical experience in Parliament gave him a particularly sharp insight into political behavior. This letter is an early statement of Spengler's underlying theme, of that of Ortega y Gasset's *Revolt of the Masses,* and of many more recent expositions of the danger of the cult of the lowest common denominator. If there should grow up in this continent a generation of men and women ready to give their lives to defending the last strongholds of the practice of individual liberty, their first duty would be to prove, by word and deed, that Macaulay and Spengler and Ortega y Gasset were wrong. The imperative need of our time is to prove to ourselves first, and to the rest of the world after, that the methods of self-government can assure elbow room to the individual man in an industrial society.

A solution to the problem would be seemingly hopeless if new factors had not appeared which Macaulay had no way of foreseeing. One is the immense increase in productivity. Another is the mass distribution of mass-produced goods which has resulted from high wages. Macaulay had no way of knowing that the American industrialist and the American farmer would be producing within a hundred years such a profusion of goods that the problems facing our political economy would be those of surplus rather than scarcity. Whenever we get a breathing space from the waste of war, we start to pile up such mountains of wheat and corn, such rivers of crude oil, such avalanches of automobiles, washing machines, hedge clippers, of everything you can think of, that the economy gets the blind staggers.

Franklin Roosevelt's New Deal revolution had all the earmarks of the sort of uprising Macaulay anticipated with so much dread. We had our hundreds and thousands of artisans out of work. We had our mutinous and discontented labor. "Tax, tax, tax. Spend, spend, spend. Elect, elect, elect" was the watchword. The sufferers marched to the polls and elected and re-elected Franklin Roosevelt who sure ranted about the tyranny of capitalists and bankers. The rich were despoiled through the income tax. The poor were to a certain extent subsidized. But the end result, instead of the republic's being laid waste by the barbarians from below, was that nearly everybody got richer, at least in material things.

Nobody who remembers what these United States looked like in the nineteen-twenties can drive across the country today without seeing the spread of electric power, the improvement in roads, in school buildings, in the health of the children you see in the playgrounds, in all kinds of housing, in all the facilities for more comfortable living. The people of this country are richer in material goods than they were thirty years ago and that wealth is very much more evenly distributed.

Events have disproved Macaulay's theory that wealth is unsafe in any hands but those of the rich. It is as untenable as the complementary theory that taking their wealth away from the rich adds to the well-being of the poor. Wealth, in modern industrial society, would seem to lie in the full use of technology and know-how to produce goods, and in seeing to it that the men who produce them get enough return for their effort to be able to buy and enjoy the goods they help to make. At the same time the intellectual leveling which has come about through mass communication would seem to have left the workingman, in an industrial structure so cut up into segments that no man can see beyond the end of his nose, neither more nor less capable than the businessman or the farmer of dealing with political problems.

Though the first results of mass communication, as of mass education, have been to level thinking to a lowest common denominator set pretty near the idiot level, it is possible to hope that the eventual results will be immensely to broaden the educated class "deeply interested in the security of property and the maintenance of order," to whose hands Macaulay wished to entrust the supreme power.

On the other hand, future historians are going to puzzle over the fact that just at the moment when American industrial society was showing how youthful and elastic it was, and how adaptable to changing conditions, so many well-educated young men threw overboard the whole idea of self-government within a framework of law, and turned to the Communist Party. They are going to puzzle about our failure as a nation to draw any advantage for ourselves or for the world from a series of military victories in the course of two world wars. At the moment when our traditional social values were proving their practical effectiveness the underlying ethical structure was showing every sign of coming apart at the seams.

Somewhere along the way we lost our conviction that the best government was self-government. In our enthusiasm for turning over every social problem to the administrative bureaucracy for solution, we forgot that democracy is based on the maxim that the solution of the problems of social life is the business of the people themselves. Neither Macaulay nor Jefferson, when they scanned the horizon for dangers threatening American democracy, foresaw this prodigious growth of a bureaucracy armed with police powers, a bureaucracy which bids fair to become a vested interest in its own right.

The whole subject has been confused, of course, by the doubletalk of the zealots for total bureaucratic rule, a doubletalk where the old vocabulary of democratic liberties is made to mean something wholly different from what was originally intended; but the fact remains that Americans are finding it harder and harder to apply the words and phrases that fitted so well the society that Jefferson and Madison lived in, to the pyramidal social structures of today.

Man is an institution-building animal. The shape of his institutions is continually remolding his life. Every new process for the production of food and goods, or for their distribution, changes the social structure. Careers are tailored to fit each new process. People's lives become intertwined with the complicated structures of vested interests. With every institutional change adaptations are demanded. Adaptation is slow and difficult and painful. The symptoms of insufficient adaptation are maladjustment, frustration, and apathy. The bureaucratic social structure that has grown up round the present type of industrial production has developed so fast that we are finding it hard, perhaps harder than we realize, to operate the system of checks and balances against inordinate power which the English-speaking people built up through centuries of resistance to authority.

It was Jefferson's sarcastic young friend from Orange County, little James Madison, who set down, in the often-quoted number 51 of the *Federalist*, the basic hardheaded rule on which all the men of the generation of 1776, radical and conservative alike, based their political theories: "In framing a government which is to be administered by men over men, the great difficulty lies in this; you must first enable the government to control the governed and in the next place oblige it to control itself."

The first problem which men will face, when they try to make elbow room for themselves and for their fellows in the new type of society now coming into being, will be the problem of bureaucracy. Bureaucracy has become dominant in government, in industry, and in the organizations of labor. The first interest of these bureaucracies, as of all human institutions, is in their own survival. If these bureaucratic hierarchies, which seem unavoidable in a mass society, can be harnessed to the dynamic needs of self-government, the task of reversing the trend towards individual serfdom into a trend towards individual liberty may not be as hard as it seems at the first glance.

The first prerequisite is a fresh understanding, untrammeled by prejudice or partisan preconceptions, of the instiutions we live *in*. Such a view is unlikely to result from the labors of research teams or sponsored surveys. The prime discoveries are more likely to be made by solitary individuals, who have managed by hook or crook to find the elbow room they need to look about them, and the self-sufficiency they need to observe their world objectively.

Observing objectively demands a sort of virginity of the perceptions. A man has to clear all preconceived notions out of his head in a happy self-forgetfulness where there is no gap between observation and description.

There's a description of a variety of cuttlefish in Darwin's *Voyage of the Beagle* that gives a notion of the delights of firsthand observation:

> Although common in pools of water left by the retiring tide these animals are not easily caught. By means of their long arms and suckers they could drag their bodies into very narrow crevices; and when thus fixed, it required great force to remove them. At other times they darted tail first, with the rapidity of an arrow, from one side of the pool to the other, at the same instant discoloring the water with a dark chestnut brown ink. These animals can also escape detection by a very extraordinary chameleonlike power of changing their color. They appear to vary their tints according to the nature of the ground over which they pass; when in deep water, their general shade was brownish purple, but when placed on land their dark tint changed into one of yellowish green. The color, examined more carefully, was a French grey, with numerous minute spots of bright yellow: the former of these varied in intensity, the latter entirely disappeared and appeared again by turns. These changes were effected in such a manner that clouds, varying in tint between a hyacinth red and a chestnut brown were continually passing over the body.

The sensitivity of a man's perceptions is in no way increased by the squinting of eyes and the straining of ears. The state of mind of the dispassionate observer is somewhat analogous to the hunter's. An expert hunter in a duck blind, or walking behind his dogs round the edges of a cornfield or waiting by a deerpath in the woods, thinks of nothing. He forgets himself. He lets all his senses come awake to respond to the frailest intimations that come to his ears or his eyes of the movement of game. Really good shots, the fellows who really bring down the quail, are people who are able to forget who they are and become for the moment just an eye and an ear and a gun.

To report objectively some scene, some situation, the movement of some animal, the shape of some organism under the microscope, a man has to fall into a state of unpreoccupied alertness very similar to the state of a sharpshooter stretched out under cover to take a bead on an enemy.

This hunter or sharpshooter knows what to look for. For years he has been building up a bank of experience. A good ornithologist can give one glance into a thicket where I see only some English sparrows and pick out a wren sitting on her nest, and three different kinds of warblers. As a result of a lifetime of observation a good hunter can tell, from the slightest disturbance of twigs and pinetags on a path through the woods, whether it was a deer or a raccoon that just passed that way.

The trouble with most classroom education is that the emphasis is on the name of the thing instead of on the thing itself. Classroom education teaches men to believe that if they have labeled and pigeonholed something they have disposed of it. So the educated man is liable to start to apply the label before he has really seen the object. To describe something objectively you have to see the individual thing before you name it.

Of course where the uneducated man falls down is in integrating what he has seen into some rational scheme. He's likely to try to fit the picture into some purely superstitious frame. Still, before you have an experience or an event fresh and new and individual enough to be worth integrating into your rational scheme, you've got, just for a slice of a second, to let yourself fall into the uneducated man's naive and ignorant frame of mind. Astonishment is a wonderful stimulus to thought.

You have to meet each new phenomenon with a clean slate as if you had never heard of it before. Most of the time we live in a shut-in universe of labels and classifications and verbalisms. It's only in brief glimpses that we have the luck to see things as they are, instead of as we were told they ought to be.

I wonder sometimes if the curiosity that makes a man want to see clearer and clearer isn't related to the hunters' or trackers' alertness, which might well have been one of the qualities most needed for survival far back in the history of the race.

The state of mind that makes for objective description, like every state of mind in which you forget who you are, has a sort of primeval happiness about it. You look out at the world with a fresh eye as if it were the morning of the first day of creation.

There is a lucid little paragraph in a translation from the original Latin of William Harvey's *Circulation of the Blood:*

> We have a small shrimp in these countries, which is taken in the Thames and in the sea, the whole of whose body is transparent; this creature, placed in a little water, has frequently afforded myself and particular friends an opportunity of observing the motions of the heart with the greatest distinctness, the extreme parts of the body presenting no obstacle to our view, but the heart being perceived as though it had been seen through a window.

Before we can start even to suggest the readjustments needed to assure fresh elbow room for the individual we must manage to see the shape of our society as clearly as Harvey saw the heart of the shrimp.

Essay Two

Some Biological Aspects of Individualism

Conway Zirkle

Conway Zirkle (1895–1972) received his Ph.D. from Johns Hopkins and studied from 1925 to 1930 as a National Research Council Fellow at Harvard University. He came to the University of Pennsylvania as associate professor of botany in 1930, advanced to professor in 1937, and retired as emeritus professor in 1966. His interests included genetics, plant cytology and the history of science. He was the author of The Beginnings of Plant Hybridization, Death of a Science in Russia *and* Evolution, Marxian Biology and the Social Scene. *He also was coauthor (with Marius J. Sirks) of* The Evolution of Biology.

On November 24, 1959, an even century will have elapsed since the first publication of Charles Darwin's great work, *The Origin of Species.*

No other book of the nineteenth century made so great an impact on the thinking of our times and no other biologist has ever placed the human species so securely and so accurately into its natural setting. Soon after the *Origin* appeared, Sir Charles Lyell and Thomas Henry Huxley published more detailed accounts of human evolution and, a little later, Darwin himself focused his attention on the origin of the human race. This application of the doctrine of evolution to human beings brought us face to face with our own species and put us in a position where we could gain a better knowledge of ourselves. Such knowledge is indispensable if we are to understand what kind of creatures we really are and what we must do to improve our lot.

Since these early pioneers placed *Homo sapiens* in his proper cosmic niche, their successors have made new and important discoveries, which both verify and supplement the original contributions. Today we know definitely that we belong in the world of nature and that it is possible to explain our advent through the operation of natural processes.

In the middle of the nineteenth century, however, the idea that mankind might be only an accidental product of the interaction of inanimate forces was very unsettling and very naturally started controversy. The disputes which followed in the wake of *The Origin of Species* led to much confusion and some acrimony. Perhaps no other scientific work has ever been misunderstood so frequently, and perhaps no other series of misunderstandings has ever persisted so disastrously. The theory of evolution penetrates to the very core of our being. It deals with the fundamental aspects of our existence, our character, and our behavior. No part of us can escape its impact or its application. We are as we are because of the way our species has evolved in the past, and we shall be as we shall be because of the course our future evolution takes.

From the very first, it was clear that if man has evolved he must belong to an unstable and changing species; a species, moreover, that had existed for ages in many different environments; one that had lived under many and diverse conditions. It was just as clear that the ancestors of the human stock had been able to survive their past vicissitudes only by adapting themselves to the different circumstances as they arose. In view of this history, extending back to the very dawn of life, it seemed rather silly for the human race to seek anywhere for permanence or security. Certainly it seemed futile for any such race to devise for itself any absolute systems of behavior or to search the universe for absolute ethical codes or moral standards—or even for codes which contain merely *ad hoc* directives for ethical contingencies.

Thus the acceptance of evolution had logical consequences in many fields. It did not take the thinking fraction of our species long to realize that it would be well for us to learn how evolution works and to adapt ourselves to the process, if we thought our well-being desirable or even that our species should continue to exist. Moreover, it was soon apparent that we could not call a halt to the process, but would continue to evolve even if we made no effort to alter or direct the course of our future evolution. Obviously no species as variable as ours can ever stop evolving, no matter how much it tries. Evolution is clearly a natural process inherent in life itself, and evolution will continue as long as life lasts. Under any and all circumstances then, the human race will be altered as time passes—in fact, as long as it survives—but it might not change in a desirable direction.

One consequence of this newer knowledge, however, was very cheering. The fact that we had become aware of our own evolution allowed us to participate in the process and even made our participation mandatory. Insight into our biological history was bound to affect our standards and our behavior, and these, in turn, would affect the conditions under which we live—affect the surroundings in which we shall evolve. Some of the more optimistic of the nineteenth-century thinkers even proposed that we take over the management of our own evolution and channel it toward some preconceived goal. Today we know that we are not entirely the masters of our fate, certainly not the captains of our souls, but neither are we innocent and passive bystanders. Many factors in nature interact to cause and direct our evolution, but our understanding of evolution has itself become one of the factors.

By this time it may be asked why a paper, in a symposium on "Individuality and Personality," should begin by calling attention to some elementary aspects of human evolution. The answer is to be found both in the theory of evolution itself and in the history of our knowledge of the subject. Indeed, practically all of our present-day attitudes toward ourselves both as individuals and as members of society—our attitudes toward individualism as contrasted with collectivism—toward the common man and the uncommon man, have been modified by one role or another that we have assigned to the individual man in the evolution of his species. Many of our present-day attitudes toward individuality predate our knowledge of evolution, but none of them has escaped the influence of evolutionary thinking.

It is perhaps fortunate that the nineteenth-century evolutionists did not agree as to the role of the individual in evolution, because a premature or erroneous conclusion, if universally accepted, might have affected our action disastrously. As we know now, the earlier explanations of evolution, while clear, logical, and complete, were not all true; and actions based on false premises more often than not have lamentable consequences. At the time of Darwin, no single explanation of evolution would fit all the known facts and evolution could be explained only by combining several of the current hypotheses.

Again fortunately, the two leading hypotheses assigned roles to the individual which were diametrically opposed, and this made it possible for each hypothesis, if used properly, to check the extremes of the other, but —and this time unfortunately—they were rarely so used. When the educated guesses of the biologists spread into the public domain, many of the complexities were lost and the interactions and the buffering effects of the hypothetical causes of evolution were missed. One or another type of simplification preempted one or another ideology and, today, the effects of these ancient simplicisms are still with us, and still infect our climate of opinion.

As is usual in such cases, the overly simplified doctrines were extended until they reached some rather unintelligent extremes. Individuals, as such, especially very able individuals, were assigned important but contradictory roles in society, roles that ranged all the way from glorious hero to depraved villain. The rugged individual *qua* individual was looked upon by some as an exemplary model of the future man, who would lead us to the dawn of a new day, and by others as a horrible example of a reactionary atavism, as a man who stood squarely against all humanitarian progress. The doctrine of evolution, however, was not solely responsible for the divergent views as to the proper role of the individual in society. The intellectual ferment of the early nineteenth century had already focused attention on the subject.

Since the middle of the eighteenth century, there had been growing appreciation of the value of personal liberty and gradual recognition of the fact that intellectual freedom not only adds to human dignity and importance but that it also is prerequisite for human progress. The whole picture, however, was neither simple nor clear. There had been some spectacular abuses of popular liberty—more emergent savagery than the forward-lookers would admit—and some of the consequences of free thought had brought confusion to well-tested codes of conduct. Ancient abuses, it is true, were being cured, but a number of the best loved and most highly respected beliefs were being challenged.

In spite of the clash of contradictory opinions and

the more than average amount of intellectual confusion that existed at the time of Darwin, the stage
was well set for an appreciation of the value of exceptionally able individuals. Individual enterprise in business was rapidly improving the lot of mankind. The
freeing of business from its medieval shackles had allowed it to grow spectacularly. To many thinkers it
seemed that, if some freedom from governmental restraint were good, more would be better. In fact, some
even held that the least possible restraint would be
best. The doctrine of *laissez faire* had become respectable and popular except to some conservatives—to
most liberals it even seemed axiomatic. Herbert Spencer and Walter Bagehot went so far as to give it a
cosmic backing by tying it into the principles of evolution. Indeed, *laissez faire* was looked upon as a necessary condition for any rational economic system—an
economic system compatible with nature. And, of
course, all human conventions and conduct had to be
"natural" if they were to be valid—if they were to be
suitable for a species which had evolved in nature.
Mankind had reached its present dominance over all
other forms of life through evolution and, according
to Darwin, evolution had come about through the
process of natural selection—through success in the
struggle for existence. The more advanced thinkers of
the period, the then contemporary progressives, even
believed that, within human society, this natural selection—this struggle for existence—should take the form

of business competition in an economy that was completely free. This extension of natural selection into human society is now called social Darwinism, a doctrine that practically dominated economic thinking during the latter part of the nineteenth century.

On the other hand, some of the evils of unrestrained business competition were too spectacular to be hidden and it was requiring more and more talent on the part of the social Darwinians to ignore them. Others did not wish to ignore, but sought rather to emphasize and even to exaggerate them. Some few even looked upon competition itself as inherently evil. If many able individuals, when free to exercise their superiority, could and did profit at the expense of their more stupid brothers, then the natural way to prevent such exploitation seemed to be to lessen freedom, the theory being that the more such individuals can be forced to conform to the standards of the masses, the less they can harm society. Some humanitarians even looked upon the masses themselves as the most important component of humanity because they were the most numerous. So a simple and easily remembered slogan, "the greatest good to the greatest number," became the goal of many reformers.

The communism of Karl Marx professed to have this objective and, as its ostensible purpose, it developed a program for equalizing the status of all individuals. Communism set as its goal an equalitarian society, a society wherein all men would be equal, not only in law and in their privileges and natural rights, but even in their biological potentialities. According to Marx's limited understanding of evolution, the biological equipment of all men could be made equal in a generation or so and, once equalized, the inherent ability of every individual could be kept the same. When this goal was reached, society, free from all such disturbing factors as personal ambition in its members would, supposedly, run itself automatically and effectively, and soon the state itself with all its governmental functions would "wither away." The state, having served its purpose in a barbarous world, would vanish and be no longer needed in the glorious, classless world of the future. *Laissez faire* was actually reentering the social structure but this time through the back door, brought in by Marx himself.

The individualistic theoreticians of unrestrained business competition and the collectivistic Marxian Communists had both developed their ideologies before Darwin published *The Origin of Species,* before anything at all was known about human evolution or of its relevance to social ideals. But when they learned that mankind had come into being through natural processes, they lost little time in applying the newly discovered knowledge to their political and economic theories. The applications, however, were highly selective and far from complete. Both sets of doctrinaires accepted only that portion of evolution theory that was compatible with their ideal systems of society and they ignored or trimmed away all the rest until the theory of evolution was reduced to a doctrine that would fit the preconceived programs of reform.

Evolution, as we know, is a complex process, too complex in fact to fit into any simplistic scheme for improving mankind. At first, however, most of those who accepted the theory did not recognize its complexity. Few even saw it as a whole and, to make matters worse, practically everyone accepted a number of beliefs that we now know to be false. At the time, nothing was easier than for zealots of many kinds to pick and choose the hypotheses that they liked, and to mold, from their gleanings, a doctrine to suit their hearts' desires. Some of these doctrines are still with us and still influence our collective thinking although, today, their fundaments rest on nothing firmer than vested ignorance. But to understand these doctrines we shall have to examine their origins.

Darwin called his great book *The Origin of Species by Means of Natural Selection, etc.* and he explained evolution by ascribing to nature the ability to preserve certain types which had arisen fortuitously and to discard others. Nature achieved this by means of an enormous overproduction of young, and she followed this excessive production by a selective death rate. Malthus had noted this overproduction long before

Darwin, and Darwin admitted that he got the idea from Malthus, but Malthus had never recognized the fact that the death rate could be selective—that it could be different for different types.

The individuals who were better adapted to their surrounding conditions survived in nature and were defined as the fit, and these fit lived and begat their kind in contrast to the unfit who perished and left no offspring. If evolution were a good thing, and the speeding up of its operation a worthy activity, then helping the fit to survive was an act of virtue; but this virtue would be lost if the same assistance were extended to the unfit. Indeed, without the nonsurvival of the unfit, evolution would be blocked. Consequently, to assist the unfit not to survive was an activity that made for evolutionary progress. Here, then, was justification for a type of individualism which was antithetical to the traditional Christian virtues and, indeed, to most of the ethical codes of mankind.

Now there is no avoiding the fact that nature is often brutal, that tragedy in nature is not unusual, and that evolutionary progress often results from a vicious combat, a struggle for existence. These facts had long been known, but most people were happier when they were thinking about something else. Tennyson, however, had faced the cruelties of nature with courage, and in 1855, four years before the *Origin of Species* was published, had written in *Maud:*

> The Mayfly's torn by the swallow,
>   the sparrow spear'd by the shrike.
> And the whole little wood where I sit
>   is a world of plunder and prey.

Consistently, a character in his later playlet, *The Promise of May* (1882), declaimed:

> And if my pleasure breeds another's pain,
> Well—is not that the course of nature too?

The philosophers also were aware that nature ignored their humanitarian thought. In 1819, just forty years before the *Origin* was published, Schopenhauer had compared the suffering of an animal being eaten with the pleasure of the animal doing the eating, concluding that the pain outweighed the pleasure. Thus the stage was set for a quick understanding of the moral implications of natural selection, although, as we shall see, the understanding was defective. Today we can appreciate the dilemma of the nineteenth-century evolutionists—humane individuals to a man—when, without meaning to, they seemed to give support to a barbaric ethical system.

A full discussion of the problem is not feasible here, but we may give our passing attention to two of its results. First, we can trace back to a perversion of this code the horrors of both the recent and existing concentration camps and the attempts of "superior races" to despoil the "inferior" ones. Second, we can attribute to the harshnesses of the code the weakminded escapism of those who would remove mankind from the biological world. But both the savagery and the escapism are based on misunderstandings of oversimplifications of a sound scientific principle. They both overlook the fact that the traditional virtues do exist and are widely distributed. This existence of the virtues means that the virtues themselves are fit and owe their continued existence to the fact that they aid the survival of those individuals who practice them. Their existence can be justified by nature just as the existence of any other property of living matter can be justified and, at this point, we come to the very heart of the biological relationship of the individual to his group.

The nature of the behavior patterns which evolve into what we call virtues depends upon the nature of the units which have been successful in the struggle for existence. For animals, who live alone and are selected as separate individuals, the egotistical traits are good. The lone wolf, however, is not in a very strong position. Gregariousness has survival value because animals who gang up are generally able to kill their competitors who do not. When animals live together in groups, nature generally selects the group as a unit as well as the separate individuals who make up the group. The group as a whole is either fit or unfit. The strength of the strong then becomes the strength of the group. Thus the characteristics which will enable the group to survive have seen selected, and among these characteristics is the ability to cooperate.

Now, in a group, altruistic characteristics have top survival value, for without them, the group could not exist. A harmonious group that has developed a high degree of team play—all for one and one for all—can generally defeat any pack of prima donnas. Even the self-sacrifice of an individual may be justified biologically if it enables his group to survive. The civilized custom of saving "women and children first" in an emergency or time of danger is both an act of virtue and sound biology. Indeed its virtue can be explained by the fact that it *is* sound biologically. Groups composed of what we consider decent citizens are actually stronger than those composed of the self-centered and the uncooperative. Any behavior pattern that helps to preserve a species represents, for that species, the highest virtues. Thus natural selection accounts for the present existence of both the egotistic and the altruistic traits. In an effective species these traits will be kept in proper balance. Too much egotism and the individual may become a vicious criminal, too much altruism and he becomes a ready-made victim for exploitation. Both egotism and altruism are selected by nature.

Natural selection, we know today, is a major factor in evolution. Together with mutation pressure and a chance loss of genes (in small populations) it explains how evolution takes place. When natural selection first made its impact on ethical theory, however, mutation pressure was an unknown factor and the very existence of the genes was not suspected. Without these ancillary factors, natural selection could not explain evolution completely. But, fortunately for the peace of mind of the evolutionists, if not for the accuracy of their conclusions, there was another explanation of evolution that supplemented natural selection to perfection and the two hypotheses together accounted for all the known facts.

This second supposed cause of evolution was known as "the inheritance of acquired characters," a doctrine that had been accepted generally for well over two thousand years. Not until late in the nineteenth century was its validity questioned seriously. Then the critical experiments, designed to test its validity, gave negative results and these experiments, incidentally, were made by the thousands. Also, the growing knowledge of biology became incompatible with the notion that acquired characters were inherited, and now the belief has been abandoned by all honest and critical biologists. During the time when it was a respectable hypothesis, however, it had a real influence upon the educated laity.

The doctrine of the inheritance of acquired characters, like that of natural selection, also assigned two divergent roles to the individual in the evolution of his species. If the characteristics that an individual acquires during his life can be transmitted to his progeny, then his experiences and the effects of environment upon him assume a genetic importance. All living conditions which improve him as an individual would also improve his progeny, hence also his species. In addition, the transmission of acquired characters would furnish a technique for securing a real biological equality of all individuals. That is, an altruistic concern by the exceptionally able for the welfare of their less fortunate fellows, giving every possible advantage to the backward and the stupid fraction of mankind, would, in time, make these depressed human specimens equal to the best.

Once equality were reached, the whole population could move forward as a unit and everyone would evolve in the same direction and, with very little social adjustment, at the same rate. No longer need evolution depend upon an elite fraction of a species superseding the mass of the mediocre, only to be superseded in turn by a new and superelite. "From each according to his ability, to each according to his needs" could, under these conditions, be the slogan of a rapidly evolving and improving species. Thus it is not remarkable that the present Communists, as well as those others who get their intellectual directives from Marx and Engels, accept the inheritance of acquired characters as an article of faith.

But another and antithetical application of the doctrine can also be made and the two applications are so far apart that men as philosophically and ethically antagonistic as Karl Marx and Herbert Spencer could both incorporate the doctrine into their systems of thought. According to this second view, the successful social Darwinian (or rather Spencerian) competitor, by grabbing the best of everything and retaining a disproportionate share, could assure that his children would have "the most of the best" and, strengthened by their superior environment, they would be in a better position to grab for themselves and for their own children and so on, as long as evolution lasted. In such a system "he should take who has the power and he should keep who can" and this taking and keeping would ensure evolutionary progress.

When we look back upon the intellectual ferment of the nineteenth century, we can hardly fail to see the influence that the then current biological theories exerted upon the more advanced thinking of the period. It is hardly astonishing that both the authoritarian and the liberal systems, which jelled at the time, include within themselves one or another of the explanations of evolution. And any system which required the stability of a religion would naturally retain the explanation. Today, communism still accepts *in toto* the biological line set by Marx and Engels. We are all aware of the recent outlawing of genetics in the Communist world and of the limited partisan acceptance of Darwin's contributions by the Communists, even though in their universities they teach courses in what they call "Darwinism."

Biology today has as much relevance to our social problems as it ever had. We still live in a biological world no matter what we may do to avoid it, and the only way we can leave the biological world is to die. Of course, we do not live only in a biological world. We are gregarious and live in society—in a social world—but this social world cannot exclude the biological as long as the individual members of society breathe, eat and reproduce themselves biologically. Consequently, all attempts to exclude the biological factors from social thought will fail whenever the thinking is honest, and all that such attempts accomplish is to call attention to the thinker's escapism. The biological and evolutionary factors, however, often affect us indirectly —through our society and within the milieu of our cultural environment. Now, at last, we can observe their indirect action and evaluate the complex interplay of the biological and the social factors; an interaction, incidentally, which has played a major role in human evolution.

Unfortunately, evolution has become a very technical and complicated subject. This has removed it from the field of general education and thus from the intellectual equipment of the generality. Many even of our better educated fellow citizens are quite innocent of any knowledge of the subject. We know today that evolution cannot be understood by anyone who is ignorant of genetics, systematics (of both living and extinct life forms), and even of mathematics.

Evolution is possible only through a differential reproductive and survival rate—only through the survival of the fit. In our species, the fit are those best suited for living in human society. It would be well to emphasize, however, that there is nothing absolute about evolutionary fitness. The fittest are merely those who survive in greater numbers under the existing conditions and who reproduce their type more successfully than their rivals reproduce theirs. When conditions change, a different complex of characters may constitute fitness.

Human culture is *the* major factor that determines which types of individuals are the fit and which are the unfit. But human culture always passes into the custody of those it selects. If *they* cannot preserve the culture, then the culture itself becomes unfit and perishes. Our histories show one collapse of culture after another and, when a culture falls, it is always replaced by some simpler system which seems better suited to the type of citizen selected by it. This interaction of biological and cultural changes constitutes a feedback mechanism and now we have evidence that such a feedback mechanism —though one working opposite to the one described here—was responsible for human beings evolving so rapidly away from and beyond all their simian relatives. The feedback interactions of our cultural and our biological evolution have made our species truly unique. No other species ever experienced such a complex cultural and biological interaction, because no other species ever developed such a complex culture to act as an agent of biological selection.

In this, our human evolution, the individual plays a dual role. Evolutionary progress occurs only when the biological reproduction of superior individuals exceeds that of the mediocre. But this reproduction can occur only under certain cultural conditions—only in a culture which demands superior qualities in those who live and leave offspring. In our past evolutionary history, these conditions have arisen continuously as human culture became more complex and this ever-growing complexity has been brought about in turn through the personal activities of superior individuals. Once we recognize that our culture is the chief agency in nature that selects us, we can readily grasp the fact that individuals who change or modify our culture actually contribute to and modify our biological evolution.

But before we can trace further this role of the exceptional individual in our evolution, we will have to determine what it is that produces such individuals, and this brings us to the modern science of genetics. We will have to glance for a moment at the machinery of our heredity. We know that our species is extremely heterozygous and this means that human beings do not breed "true." Sometimes, musicians beget musicians, poets beget poets, and scientists beget scientists. These instances, however, are rare and are due to many factors. Outstanding men more often than not have fathers who are not particularly outstanding. Genetically we are much like our hybrid corn, which does not duplicate its own exceptional virtues in its progeny, and we are also like our fruit trees that do not breed true from seed. Many of our geniuses have children but nearly always the children are only "seedlings." If we could reproduce our truly great men vegetatively, as we do our fruit trees, we could, of course, have them in almost any number.

A word of warning is indicated at this point. The fact that practically no human beings breed "true" is no indication at all that men are equal biologically or that the progeny of different men have equal potentialities. We know now that the opposite is the case. Here we will merely state that large, heterozygous populations continually produce extreme Mendelian segregants and that our great men—our exceptionally able fellows—are such segregants. At this point we are concerned merely with the role of such human segregants in altering the biological potentialities—altering the gene frequencies—of the stocks that produced them.

The total number of such segregants may be minute when compared with the millions of individuals within the whole population but, over the years, such segregants will be numerous. They will also deviate from the norm of the population in all recognizable ways. Many segregants will not meet with conditions suitable for the development of their peculiar talents and they will have to remain mute and inglorious—also guiltless. Some few, however, will fall into a favorable milieu and will become historical characters; become great heroes or great villains. Some will even affect the course of history, of culture, of society itself. These are the segregants who actually become factors in evolution.

The acknowledgment of the role of the extreme Mendelian segregant might seem superficially to be an endorsement of the Great Man theory of history. Actually it is not. The Great Man theory of Carlyle can be shown to be as inadequate as all other monophyletic theories. The extreme Mendelian segregant is a factor, however, and an important one, but it is only one factor among many. Our only concern here is to examine the manner in which such great men alter our culture and thus, indirectly, our biological evolution. A few examples will make the process clear.

The inventor of the bow and arrow undoubtedly gave his group or tribe an enormous advantage in the struggle for existence. The power of shooting greatly augmented the efficiency of the hunters and, thus, the food supply. This led to an increased population. As a military weapon, the bow and arrow gave the people who possessed it the ability to expand at the expense of their competitors. Whether the bow was invented only once, or many times, makes no real difference. In either case, during the period between invention and spread, it gave a different survival value to those tribes which had it from those that did not. The number of people in some tribes would increase but in others decrease, and this could produce changes in gene frequencies over large areas.

Such examples as the invention of the bow could

be cited indefinitely. The great technical advances
made in Europe during the fifteenth, sixteenth, and
seventeenth centuries are cases in point. They increased greatly the power of the Europeans both to
expand into other continents and to grow more food
in Europe itself. They thus increased the number of
people of European stock and, in so doing, altered the
genic endowment of the human race.

All extreme human segregants, of course, are not
beneficial to the society that produces them. The particular combination of genes which grew up to be
known as Adolf Hitler, appearing just when it did and
under prevailing circumstances, had an evolutionary
significance which did not help its tribe at all. It probably altered permanently the ratio of Teuton to Slav.
Likewise, the little group of men who seized control
of Russia has also changed the populations, and hence
the genic frequencies, in many stocks over a large portion of the globe. The store of genes of the Baltic nations may well have been depleted in part through the
extermination of their leaders and their professional
and educated classes. (The extermination of local
leaders is, of course, a recognized technique of establishing a foreign hegemony.) Many other effects of
communism upon biological evolution can be cited,
such as those produced by forced migrations and re-
settlement, and by the liquidating of whole social
classes. The differential butchery of "bourgeois" Chinese by those now in power may well have altered the

genic endowment of the Chinese race. Another form of totalitarianism also had its evolutionary effects in the Hitlerian concentration camps—camps which lowered the genic endowment of the world.

The role of the extreme Mendelian segregant in evolution, however, should not be overemphasized. It is only one factor in a complex equation and certainly not the most important factor. It is, however, an erratic variable and the complexity of its functioning is so great that the effects can never be calculated with any certainty. We can never tell in advance when a Mendelian segregant might initiate a major change in human affairs and consequently in the genic reservoir of the surviving population. At some time in the future, some new religion may appear, some "holy" war may be fought or some new fanaticism or ideology may break loose and destroy a portion of mankind. Some few of the future Pied Pipers will certainly have enough followers to become worldwide nuisances and some may even affect the future of our species. Do what we will, this erratic factor in evolution—this factor due to the activities of individuals who are extreme Mendelian segregants—will always be with us and will always defy our best prognostications.

The role of the exceptionally able individual in our cultural and biological evolution thus is not too difficult to discover. But the discovery does not give us a complete picture. We still have to investigate the factors which produce such individuals.

Before we can proceed with this task, however, we should dispose of a completely bogus problem—that of heredity *vs.* environment. As we know, statements made in the past that either heredity or environment is more important than the other are without meaning. To consider one as more important than the other in producing any single individual is as meaningless as considering the multiplier more important than the multiplicand (or the reverse) in deriving a product. Both heredity and environment are conditions of life and both have an absolute veto power over all individual human achievement. Detailed evidence for this statement cannot be given here but the evidence is available to anyone who wishes to secure it.

The exceptionally able individuals—those whose cumulative and cooperative efforts have created our culture and who now direct and control our collective acts—have never formed more than a minute fraction of our species. Moreover, they have never shown themselves able to reproduce their kind but, on the contrary, their production, in each instance, is fortuitous and their total number, at any one time, variable. Yet their continued existence is essential if our civilization is to endure and if we are to preserve the gains we have made. Certainly cultural progress is impossible without the contributions made by superior men. Thus it is only a truism to state that the continued production of superior men is a necessary condition for cultural advance in the future.

If we wish to contribute knowingly to our future well being, we shall have to identify and map the factors in our heritage that enable us to produce such able individuals. The problem before us is: How does our race manage to produce individuals who deviate so markedly from the normal? To answer this question we will have to examine the machinery of heredity.

A recent and very useful device for exploring our hereditary potential is to picture each breeding group, nation, or race as possessing a gene pool or a genic reservoir. The pool or reservoir can be considered the joint possession of the group but it does not exist in any one spot where it can be drawn upon at will. In fact it exists only in fragments—only as particular genic combinations in the germ plasm of the individuals who make up the group. Nor can the individuals release or utilize the desirable genes at will. No man even knows what genes he himself carries, though his unique individuality is a product of the unique *combination* of genes in the fertilized egg from which he developed.

Equalitarianism cannot be extended honestly to these unknown but variable combinations of genes. As we know, the various mutant forms that our genes take are not all equal. Certain forms of a gene (alleles) are far more effective than others, both in their individual functioning and in their ability to work in combinations with other genes. The frequency of these effective alleles varies enormously from population to population and also within populations, because most populations are made up of groups that are partially isolated reproductively. The frequency of the effective genes is a major factor in the value of any gene pool. Reservoirs that have many such genes produce a relatively large number of those genic combinations that can, under favorable conditions, develop into superior individuals. On the other hand, if the frequency of these genes falls too low, the gene pool may fail to produce able individuals. It may even fail to produce anyone above the mediocre.

At this point it might be well to show how the machinery of heredity produces extreme variants. This can be done most simply by the use of a completely imaginary example as an illustration. Let us assume that there are in a population ten genes whose frequency is such that each one is possessed by just half of those who make up the population. Let us suppose further that these genes are equally beneficial and that the more of them an individual has, the better off he is. Anyone who has all ten genes then would be, potentially, a very superior person. The proportion of such people in the whole population would be 2^{-10} or 1 in 1024—a little less than .1 percent. Those who had any nine of the ten genes would constitute about 1.0 percent of the population and those who had any eight would be about 4.5 percent. If the population is reasonably large, these percentages would be constant from generation to generation.

Now let us assume that this population fuses with an equal number from another population which has none of these genes at all. (Here we should repeat that this case is purely imaginary and probably applies to no human group.) The occurrence of each gene would be reduced from 50 percent of the population to 27.14 percent. (Not to 25 percent because some of the original 50 percent had a double dose of each gene.) The proportion of those who have all ten genes would be reduced from 1 in 1024 to about 1 in 461,200. The able individuals (by definition) would thus be reduced by a factor of over 450 and their number might well be reduced below that necessary to keep a civilization functioning.

This illustration is much too simple to fit anything that actually happens, because it leaves out all modifications due to selective matings. In fact, it omits all complications. But it does show how extremely susceptible all special genic combinations are to changes in the frequencies of the individual genes that compose them.

We are now in a position to examine the genetic relationship of the able and outstanding individuals to the breeding groups that produce them. All relatively rare combinations of genes—all extreme Mendelian segregants—must be heterozygous in respect to the majority of their genes, because the chance of *rare* combinations being composed of double doses of each gene is too small to be of any significance. This means that such genic combinations cannot breed true. Our able minority has such a genic formula and nearly all of them have come from parents who were not outstanding. To produce exceptionally able children it is only necessary that each parent be able to supplement the other—be able to give to the child the genes that the other parent lacks. This, incidentally, is only a special case of hybrid-vigor or, what we call "heterosis" —a recent genetical discovery that has increased so greatly the production of our corn crop.

We should emphasize, however, that even if the uncommon man arises from the commonality, all groups within the population do not produce outstanding men in equal numbers and we know enough genetics now to know that they could not do so even if all cultural variables were smoothed out and all opportunities were equalized. The extreme susceptibility of complex genic combinations to slight variations in the frequencies of individual genes would be sufficient in itself to introduce a major variable.

So we come at last to the point where we can begin to examine the all-important interaction of the biological and cultural factors that are responsible for the existence of outstanding ability. Obviously, a proper genic combination is not in itself sufficient to make a "great man." The tools of culture must also be available to him if he is to accomplish anything at all. If potentially able combinations of genes may occur throughout the greater part of the population, then the available opportunities—the tools of culture—must also be distributed throughout the population. No nation can now afford to inhibit the development of greatness in any of its potentially able. The preservation of civilization itself—not to mention its advancement—depends upon the activities of the able, and the able, in turn, owe their very existence to the masses of the mediocre who beget them. Here then is interdependence with a vengeance! Possibly the chief importance of the common man lies in the fact that, without the aid of a certain fraction of his children, we could not advance or even preserve our civilization.

One very important factor in the production of the able minority remains to be described. In the illustration we gave of the mechanism of heredity, a tacit assumption contrary to fact was made. The union of the sex cells, which produced the different combinations of genes, was assumed to be completely fortuitous, such as that which occurs in wind pollination. Human beings could secure such a fortuitous fertilization only by some artificial means such as having all the males contribute semen to a sperm bank and having all the females inseminated artificially. In the absence of such a silly practice, human reproduction will not be purely a matter of chance even though promiscuity grows and, in the dark, all cats are gray. The inevitable selective mating of human beings will affect the various combination of genes which constitute our gene pool.

While marriage is proverbially a lottery, similarity in

background, ability, taste, education, intelligence and social status are powerful selecting agents. Whenever like mates with like (genetically), the statistical distribution curve, which describes the frequency of the purely fortuitous combination of genes, is flattened out, its mode is depressed, and its extremes are increased. This reduces the number of the mediocre produced and increases the numbers of both the subnormal and the talented groups. It is possible that, without this increase in the number of the extreme variants, no nation, race, or group could produce enough superior individuals to maintain a complex culture. Certainly not enough to operate or advance a civilization.

This factor of selective mating introduces a most erratic variable into our cultural development and, over the ages, even into our biological evolution. It is itself produced by the interaction of two other variables, the two whose existence is recognized routinely, *i.e.,* heredity and environment.

We need not point out here that the character of every individual is determined by the way his biological potentialities developed in his own personal environment. We are all the product of the interaction of these two variables. But in selective mating, heredity and environment interact on still another plane. To a large extent the environment determines who marries whom and, over the generations, the product of the matings becomes a major factor in determining the all-important cultural environment. This feedback into each other of our heredity and environment acting on at least two different levels, introduces so many unmeasurable complications into our biological composition and into our cultural heritage, that our future development will remain highly unpredictable. We can be certain that our future will not be static, but that is the present limit of our certitude.

Even minor changes in our present social conventions may reduce the amount of the existing selective mating, and a marked reduction may reduce the production of the talented below some critical range. If this happens, we may expect a cultural retrogression. In the past, any number of human cultures have deteriorated and some of them have collapsed and vanished. It would be silly, of course, to ascribe the retrogressions simply to changes in the number of selective matings within the several cultures. It would be just as silly to leave this factor entirely out of our interpretations.

Any number of social customs have stood, and still stand, in the way of an optimum amount of selective matings. In a feudal society, opportunities are denied to many able men who, consequently, never develop to the high level of their biological potential and thus they remain among the undistinguished. Such able men (and women) might also be diffused throughout an "ideal" classless society and, lacking the means to separate themselves from the generality, or to develop to the full their peculiar talents, would be effectively swamped. In such a society they could hardly segregate in groups. In fact, only a few of the able males might ever meet an able female who appealed to them erotically. Obviously an open society—one in which the able may rise and the dimwits sink, a society where like levels of ability segregate out from the whole, and where like intelligences have a greater chance of meeting and mating—has advantages that other societies do not have. Our own society today—incidentally and without design—is providing more and more opportunities for intelligent matrimonial discrimination. It is possible that our coeducational colleges, where highly selected males and females meet when young, are as important in their function of bringing together the parents of our future superior individuals as they are in educating the present crop.

Today we are in an evolutionary stage where our culture is exceptionally complex, so complex in fact that it can remain effective only through the cooperative efforts of the very ablest fraction of mankind. Any change in the numbers, or competencies of these few, or any social change which would inhibit their adequate functioning, would have far-reaching consequences. These few, however, cannot reproduce themselves, and their existence in numbers sufficient to keep our culture operative depends upon Mendelian segregations from the population as a whole. The number of such individuals that any population can produce depends both upon the frequency of the individual genes which are necessary for the production of all able individuals and upon the degree of selective mating within the breeding group. These are variable factors and make for great instability.

But this is not all bad. We owe the speed and extent of our evolution to our instability. A completely stable species simply does not evolve. Instability, however, while it makes progress possible, always presents the danger of deterioration. The only certainty we now have as to our future is that it will not be stable.

Essay Three

Individuality
and Modernity

Richard M. Weaver

Richard M. Weaver (1910–1963), respected philosopher, critic and rhetorician, was professor of English at the University of Chicago. Among his books were Ideas Have Consequences *and* The Ethics of Rhetoric.

In a world which has largely accepted "modernism" as its slogan, the status of personality becomes a matter of concern to all who think reflectively and benevolently about the human being. There is an uncomfortable basis of truth in a remark I once heard made by a philosopher: as soon as something begins to disappear, we put up signs proclaiming the virtue of it. The very fact of a symposium arranged to discuss the future of individuality may be taken wryly as a sign that its prospects are poor. But sometimes men disvalue a thing only because they have forgotten how good it is comparatively. In such cases a fresh look should lead to a revival of faith and also uncover possibilities for preserving what we would be the poorer for losing.

What I understand by "individuality" is the personality vis-à-vis society and the state. Individuality is the sign of the *persona,* and it always finds its claims in the higher sanctions of the latter. Therefore, it seems necessary to say something about the true nature of personality. In what immediately follows, I shall describe a few of its aspects as they appear to an observer from the humanities. If these do not add up to a definition, at least they may help to determine in what sort of soil and climate personality, in the sense desiderated, is most likely to thrive and be respected.

It seems a threshold fact that personality is some kind of integration. The individual whom we regard as having authentic personality appears to possess a center, and everything that he does is in relation to this. When such a person performs an act, no part of his being seems uninvolved; what happens on the outer circumference is duly controlled by the integrating center. We sense, sometimes with a feeling of envy, that this individual is a unitary being and thus "in possession of himself." Of course, there are poorly integrated or disintegrated "personalities," but these we classify as unformed or degenerate just because they fall short in this property. The true personality is a psychic unity, preserving its identity and giving a sort of thematic continuity to the acts of the individual.

I have observed in many instances that different personalities possess different powers of insight into matters. A subject which is obscure to one person may be clear and understandable to another, even when the "IQ" measurement of the second is inferior to that of the first. A type of sentience open to one individual is simply closed to another. The older I grow, the more disinclined I am to disparage mental processes which at first strike me as naive, foolish, or even illogical. I can recall more than one instance in which an individual who impressed me as quite naive proved to have a better grasp of a situation than I had. Certainly some of the finest creations of civilization have been produced by persons who were regarded by their associates as simpleminded in some respects. The mysterious formula of the personality may fit the individual for unique insight and achievement in one direction while leaving him below average in others. This is the real reason for insisting that every man's view should have a chance for a respectful hearing. The Creator seems to have given different individuals different ways of cogently apprehending reality.

This selective relation of the person to the totality may suggest that personality is the final ethical tie-up of the individual. It is the special form taken by the individual in expressing the values he has recognized. When we speak of "the sacredness of the personality," as we sometimes do, we mean just this reflection through the person of ideas of the true and the good. The fact that there are as many different expressions as there are personalities need not mean that the reality is miscellaneous. It may mean rather that we are faced with a religious concept, not open to the kinds of noetic formulations that serve on other levels of knowledge. Any other conception of personality leaves it a mere aggregate of peculiarities, and the cultivation of the idiosyncratic is idiocy.

An indirect proof of this religious conception is found in the ethical maxim that the greatest wrong one can do to a person is to treat him as if he were only an instrument. To treat him as an instrument is to treat him as though he had no vision of the good to express through his particular stances and actions. There are forms of regimentation, some in labor, some in military service, and today perhaps a good many elsewhere, which the general sense regards as brutalizing because they strike down and keep suppressed any motion the individual might make toward personal discrimination and evaluation.

Our reasoning will not admit that the entire worth of a man is in his instrumental servitude. If man has a right to personality, along with the other rights that are being claimed for him today, he must have an area of freedom to express, with personal emphasis, his acknowledgment of the good. The personality is a morally oriented unit which has a duty to maintain itself against many forms of social coercion and also against the sometimes greater danger of complacence. This means a state of independence which makes the battle for personality a basic phase of the battle for freedom.

I am in agreement with those who believe that personality is on the defensive today, and I would go so far as to say that in some cases it is the object of deliberate, directed assault. That is an accusation. To justify it I shall name a few of the forces that seem to me most inimical to personality and shall discuss their impact.

There is no question that technology and industrialism are making it difficult for personality. Whatever may have been the designs of the authors of the Baconian revolution, they have produced a world in which it is increasingly hard to be human in the normative sense. Man is an organism, not a mechanism; and the mechanical placing of his life does harm to his human responses, which naturally follow a kind of free rhythm. As a small but significant illustration: I have seen an interesting conversation terminated because a member of the party remembered that the parking meter by his car had about run out.

Most of us today have to move to the sounds of bells and whistles and to changes of light; we have to keep ourselves tense so as not to miss these mechanical signals. There can be disciplinary value in a certain amount of mechanical pacing, but ours has gone too far, and servitude to the machine today involves not just those who work in factories, but the great majority. These pressures against human personality, however, are visible to all and have been much discussed, so I shall pass on to some insidious forces, which may be all the more dangerous for being subtle and sometimes concealed.

First among these is the attack upon memory. There

has never been another milieu, as far as my knowledge goes, which has sought to make forgetting a virtue. "Forget it" is a password of the time. If people make a mistake or commit a sin (to use an antiquated phrase), they are told to "Forget it." People are praised in our organs of greatest circulation for discarding all baggage of the past and conforming to a "fast-changing world." Those who live with a burden of memory are smiled at amiably, when they are not frowned upon darkly, as impediments in the way of progress. Everything is supposed to be of the moment and for the moment. In our educational programs, history, which used to be a very sobering discipline, has been dropped in favor of various scientific studies of the human record, and that passionate sense of historical reality which is at the base of much cultural achievement is actually discouraged. The mood of the individual and of the group has become ahistorical.

I cannot see this disparagement of all memory as anything but an attack upon the mind, which must have adverse effects upon the personality. According to Joseph Jastrow, "Disorders of personality involve more or less disorganization of the memory continuum and of the group of elements which enter into normal consciousness of personal identity."[1] The human being

---

[1] Joseph Jastrow, "Personality," *Baldwin's Dictionary of Philosophy and Psychology* (New York: Peter Smith, 1940), II, p. 284.

must live in a present that is enriched and sustained by a past; it is his experience stored up in the form of memory which enables him to be something more than an automaton responding to sensory impingements.

It is equally true that a man's personality is a product in large part of the memory of things he has done, decisions he has made, with their consequences, and so on. Personality cannot be the creation of a moment, for one of the things we predicate of it, with most confidence, is its uniformity. If Sam Jones is known to have a certain kind of personality, we say that in a given situation he will behave in one fashion rather than another, which might be chosen by an individual of different personality. But unless Jones carries with him a consciousness of what he has been, we can have no ground for predicting the nature of his future choices.

By the same token, without this faculty of memory there can be no such thing as conscience. Conscience is essentially a recollection or pulling together of our ideas of what we are, what the things we deal with are, and the structure of values to which we have in our inmost feelings subscribed. It is a present awareness of many things which no longer have present existence. Thus, when an individual consults his conscience, he refers to a complex of remembered facts, insights, and ideas of obligation—all of which by their very nature cannot be manufactured out of a present moment. Conscience thus requires a recollection of the self, a thinking of who and what we are before performing an act, and this is why meditation and contemplation are enjoined by most religions.

The craze for "living in the present" is related to the fact that the present is empirical time. It is the time we experience, if by experience we mean sensation. The great wave of empiricism which has engulfed modern thinking has had, as one of its logical effects, this discrediting of memory and denigration of the past. Its influence upon our very mode of thinking can be very grave.

Consider for a moment what it means to invite the individual to "live in the present." It means asking him to give up his habit of associating things, and indeed, to give up having any but the most superficial ideas. William James points out that people who remember best are those who have concept systems. A fact is rememberable when an individual is able to make "multiple associations" with it. The concept serves as a kind of frame upon which he hangs this and that item. When a particular fact is called to mind, it may suggest the framework and the framework in turn may suggest other facts.

What I particularly fear is that this attack upon memory may be a concealed attack upon all conceptualization, more especially since intellect is now regarded by a school of educational theory as "undemocratic" in its relation with the physical body. When we advise people not to remember, we may be advising them in effect not to conceptualize. In other words, "Don't think about it." Let the present trend of sensory experience determine the attitude and the decision. Today's mass journalism, with its lively propagation, its weak reflection, and its addiction to sensational data, lends powerful encouragement to the habit.

It is hard to see how this cult of forgetting, or of living entirely in the present, can avoid weakening the integration which develops personality. There is truth in the saying that a man is part of all that he has met— and I pointedly include here the choices he has made with reference to the problems that he has met. All of these experiences, active and passive, physical and intellectual, coalesce in what I have been calling his center, but what at other times has been called his soul. When the individual destroys his memory, he destroys in part his soul.

The fact that one has this kind of center means that one has created something as a result of his effort in living. And this something, resting on "the presence of the past in the present," to recall a useful phrase of T. S. Eliot's, gives one a defined character, or a self. If a man cannot remember what he did day before yesterday, how can he know what he ought to do day after tomorrow? And if, on principle, he should remember what he did day before yesterday, he should remember whatever of significance he did a year ago and five years ago, for there is no arbitrary point at which the past becomes dead.

It is even questionable whether those who claim to "live in the present" are getting more out of the present than anyone else. I agree entirely with C. G. Jung that denial of the past is by no means the same thing as consciousness of the present, and that "the really modern man is often found among those who call themselves old-fashioned."[2] This is because those who have well-stored minds are able to live more knowingly in the present. They are constantly making multiple associations, and their very erudition, which memory makes possible, becomes a means of wider sensibility. The idea of progress itself involves retrospection and accurate comparison. The pseudo-modern, who is an enemy of the past, is actually unable to understand the nature of progress.

At the same time that this pseudo-modern temper is warring against memory, it is also warring against status, with a similar harmful result to the personality. We might call it a two-pronged offensive aimed at the same goal.

I have not thoroughly tested the representation I am now going to make, but it seems to me that man is happiest (in a sense which would include spiritual happiness) when he enjoys a kind of equipoise of status and function, or of being and action. His status at any moment enables him to know what he is (or who he is)

---

[2] C. G. Jung, *Modern Man in Search of a Soul* (New York: Harcourt, Brace, 1933), p. 229.

and his function keeps him in relation with the process of human activity. In other words, the man of developed personality and achieved well-being *is* somebody and can *do* something. When these two properties are in balance in the individual, the ensuing condition can be described by that beautiful word *euphoria*.

An excessive inclination toward either status or function is upsetting. To rely wholly upon one's status, to stay wrapped up in it and suppose that it answers every need, leads to debility and sterility. It is a condition often observed in decadent aristocracies, and in any individual who has long been overprotected by status. It is not against this, however, that the present age needs warning, for its excess lies at the other end. We have gone to the extreme of attaching importance only to function, while deriding the idea of status. The current feeling is that the measure of man is what he does, and everybody is to be judged by results, like baseball players or salesmen. At first glance this has a plausible look; it seems honest whereas the other does not, and indeed there are situations in which measurement by accomplishment only is a very good corrective. We like to see presumptuous or unfounded status rebuked, and "functional" man seems to contribute more to the production of things.

A more circumspective inquiry, however, will show that the idea of status, while certainly capable of abuse, is an important element in one's psychic well-being. It is natural and it is right for a man to wish to be seen as something more than he is at a random moment. He wishes to be known as an individual, and individuality requires historicity. If he has by effort and sacrifice won himself a position among men, that position is part of his being; when you touch him, you touch it. When you address him, you are not addressing flesh; you are addressing the man within, who has achieved a *state* of being. At some point in each life, owing to the inevitable ravages of time, one's functioning efficiency is lowered. We do not subtract from the individual's honor in society because he can no longer run a hundred yards in ten seconds, or perform the labor that he could at thirty, or write poetry with the passion of his youth. Rather, his achievements are listed after his name, and he is, so to speak, emeritus.

But one of the main tendencies of modernism, if I mistake it not, is to discount accumulated status, and to insist that the only worth is that which is present and demonstrable. The philosophy of instrumentalism has lent theoretical support to this notion.

The harm that is done to the individual thereby is this: every person needs to have a sense of his place, or what is often called a sense of belonging. A sure knowledge of status, I think, confers this more than does anything else. Much of the subconscious anxiety and feeling of lostness from which many people suffer today results from this broad-scale attempt to do away with status, which is like doing away with home. Home is the place where our status is known and duly respected. Change for its own sake, and function as the sole criterion, have brought about a condition of mobility such that many people no longer feel that they have a place, physical or spiritual. I am inclined to think that pure function or activity, without a backdrop of status, is meaningless. The small boy who puts on a cowboy suit or a fireman's helmet shows that he wants to function as something.

Just as the individual requires a balance of status and function for his real happiness, so it appears that he requires a balance of outer and inner life. Part of his life has a public orientation, but part of it does not. He has a private self that looks inward, and he should be able to feel with some distinctness the difference between public and private roles. It strikes me that those eighteenth-century individuals who wrote letters to the newspapers, signed "Publius" or something like that, were giving expression to this difference. When the writer appeared before the public in the common interest, he was conscious of stepping outside his private considerations and entering into another capacity, of assuming a posture. The rest of the time he was his own man, with his thoughts and feelings reserved for himself.

Whatever barrier made this delicacy possible has long since been broken down. It is now felt that the individual's entire life is subject to public report and review. Any claim to privacy is viewed as a form of exclusiveness, to be denied in the interest of an onrushing democracy.

When a feeling becomes as pervasive as this now is, it finds many manifestations. It affects, for example, even the architecture of our houses. We have all noted the vogue of picture windows, which leave the family livingroom open to full view and appraisal of the world. Even the interiors of modern houses are so designed as to make it impossible for the individual to withdraw and find privacy. The traditional refuge of "a room of one's own," upstairs or to the rear, is no more. All must be visible and together in "the democratic way of life." Evidences like this are often more conclusive as to the real trend of mentality than what we see reflected in our newspapers and magazines.

One of the more extraordinary invasions of individual privacy is the modern income tax. I am aware that this example will appear ludicrous to some, yet I am convinced that it has a very serious side. If we take a detached view and realize the extent to which it places everybody under surveillance, we are amazed at what it assumes. I am familiar with the arguments for it on political and humanitarian grounds. What I am pointing out is that this tax makes the individual's entire economic and financial life subject to annual government audit. It is just as if we were all criminals out on parole, required once a year to file an affidavit of our doings before a public official. The fact to be pondered is that arguments against the income tax based on the right to privacy would be dismissed as trivial or irrelevant. The claim to privacy would simply not supply any leverage.

The decline of privacy is traceable, to the best of my perception, to a belief that man is or should be one-dimensional. There should be no depths, no recesses, no area of being that cannot be unfolded simply. Such a conception seems quite in line with other attempts to simplify man through various forms of scientific abstraction and to insist that he is "nothing but" a thing that these techniques of exposition can explain. If he were not that kind of thing, we might not be able to manipulate him, and this thought is anathema to the positivistic party. Since personality means depth and uniqueness, and even mystery, it does not flourish on a plane. The abolition of privacy does away with the very regions where personal configurations must form.

Possibly the worst result of this one-dimensional concept of the person is that it makes self-knowledge deceptively easy. In spite of the popularity enjoyed by psychology in recent decades, it may be questioned whether men understand themselves any better today than they did when Socrates was exhorting the Athenians to examine themselves and to learn whether man is a creature mild and gentle by nature, or a monster more terrible than Typhon. Or, one might conclude that what psychology has done to advance such understanding, political romanticism and advertising propaganda have largely undone. The pressure against the habit of contemplation and the displacement of the humanities from a central role in our education have worked against what are probably the two best means of getting to know the nature of the human being. Self-knowledge is an extremely difficult acquisition under the best circumstances, and I think no one has better expressed this truth than Eliseo Vivas:

> My experience in general inclines me to the belief that men in general live their lives through without finding out who or what they really are. We think we are courageous when we are cowards, honest when we are cheats and thieves, truthful and generous when we are liars and pigs, and self-respecting in spite of the high coefficient of pliability of our moral spines. . . . It takes a crisis to reveal to us what values we truly espouse, and even that is often not enough, for each of us has his system of jujitsu for disposing quietly of bothersome truths.[3]

If a person is satisfied with the externality of the self, and if he gathers from the tone of current thinking that personality is just so much moonshine anyhow, it is not likely that he will take pains to search out the real springs of his attitudes and actions. Actions that appear to him perfectly respectable, or even the expression of benevolence, may become the cause of

---

[3] Eliseo Vivas, *The Moral Life and the Ethical Life* (Chicago: University of Chicago Press, 1950), p. 190.

suffering to others—suffering which the agent cannot apprehend because he has a false picture of much that is involved. Such failure may become collective, and what is true of the individual in this regard may be true of the group or the nation. The same want of self-knowledge and the same self-deception regarding motives can lead nations into policies that create enmity and produce suffering. A nation, too, may have a system of jujitsu for breaking the holds of self-criticism.

I shall conclude this list of forces which are bringing about a depersonalization of the individual with one or two from the field of my professional work. Few will question the proposition that language is one of the means by which man expresses himself most personally. But in this sphere, too, we can mark the same tendencies toward oversimplification and redefinition with the apparent object of manipulating. I have in mind especially the current fondness for something called "communication." Communication is usurping the place formerly held by expression. What used to be studied as an art, with some philosophical attention to the character and resources of the user, the truth of what was being expressed, and the character of the potential audience, is now being stripped down to a technique. Many would be surprised by the extent to which this new subject is edging out the old courses in composition and rhetoric in our colleges. The significance of the change has been noted by Allen Tate in an apt sentence. "The word 'communication,' " he writes, "presupposes the victory of the secularized society of means without ends."[4]

In this paring down of expression to "communication" there are two dangerous premises. One is that communication is primarily an engineering problem, to be solved through resort to the physical science. The problem is conceived as getting certain sounds from one mouth to certain ears or of getting a set of graphic symbols before certain eyes. This reflects the obsession of the scientific linguists that language is nothing more than a code, whose ends and means can be scientifically analyzed and dealt with. The intermediate stage of encoding and decoding thus becomes the whole subject. Left out of account are the way in which language is expressive of value and personality, and the way in which the use of it shapes and disciplines the mind.

The second premise is that the object of the communication is merely a passive registrar—a pair of ears or eyes ready to absorb whatever is presented to them by our now marvelous means of transmission. I shall go into Allen Tate's debt once more, this time to quote an observation from his "Reflections on American Poetry: 1900–1950." In this *Sewanee Review* article (Winter, 1956), he notes that there are "strong political pressures which ask the poet to 'communicate'

---

[4] Allen Tate, *The Forlorn Demon* (Chicago: Henry Regnery, 1953), p. 12.

to passively conditioned persons what a servile society expects them to feel." If these forces are brought to bear upon the modern poet, they are surely brought to bear much more strongly upon the journalists and all who write for our organs of mass "communication." The extent to which they assume prior indoctrination and docility on the part of their audience is amazing when one goes to the point of analyzing it. Mass communication is not conversation, and the obstacles in the way of a meeting of speaker and hearer, in what might be termed a "man to man" or "no-nonsense" discussion, seem actually greater than ever before.

This development will suggest that loss of belief in personality is being reflected in language itself; and indeed, how else could it be if, as I. A. Richards has said, language is "the supreme organ of the mind's self-ordering growth."[5] I have to agree with F. A. Voigt that the English language today is losing character, strength, and resonance. What I am chiefly conscious of is the loss of resonance, and I think that this loss is owing mainly to the fact that the modern style shuns anything suggestive of value. Or, if this generalization must be qualified, it admits only values of the narrow, strident kind, such as might be expected to survive after positivism has done its work. There is even a theory to justify this narrowing down, as can be seen

---

[5] I. A. Richards, *Speculative Instruments* (Chicago: University of Chicago Press, 1955), p. 9.

in the curious attempts of people like Alfred Korzybski and Stuart Chase to maintain that language ought to be somehow correlated with the spatiotemporal order. Symbolism and expression of emotion are both under attack as irruptions from a nonscientific world.

If we seat a typical modern before a chapter of the King James Bible, or a passage from an eighteenth-century oration, it is problematical how much of what is there he can get. The wonderful wealth of pleonasm, metonymy, synecdoche, antithesis, isocolons, anaphoras, inversions, and climactic orders—a veritable orchestration for the soul—is, I believe, puzzling to him. His reaction, I suspect, is that the writer of the passage is saying it the best way he could, and must be pardoned, being of a primitive time. The way to say it would be in the style of *Look,* or of an editorial in the New York *Daily News,* with words of flat signification, with syncopated syntax, and with none of the broadly ruminative phrases which have the power to inspire speculation. The essential sterility of such a style is one of the surest signs we have that modern man is being desiccated. For the "modern" style is at once brash and timid; brash enough to break old patterns without thinking, and timid before the tremendous evocative and constructive powers immanent in language.

There is a temptation to suppose that by doing something to language itself we can do something about this situation. Much as I would like to think that, reason tells me that the opportunity is limited. Something will have to be done first about man's representation of himself, because that representation broadens or narrows the vocabulary and the rhetoric which he thinks he can use. But to the extent that language exerts a counter influence upon the representation, we can say that it is a causal factor, and we can do something through force of example. It is very easy to pick up unconsciously a tone, or to fall into a vocabulary, or to make use of figures and analogies, whose implications are opposite to the views we really hold. Any style moves along on a set of hidden or half-hidden premises, and there is a great if unconscious pressure to accept the premises of a style in popular use. These premises now point in the general direction of a philosophic nihilism. We cannot reinstitute the style of an age that we feel to have been more humane toward the personality, but we can, within the idiom permitted us, avoid the kind of discourse that carries just below its surface a contempt for all values.

This seems to turn the consideration toward remedial measures. One of the obvious steps, if we are to secure the future of personality, is to clarify the relation of the individual to his society.

It is quite easy to fall under the influence of our extensive literature of protest and to assume that the individual is always engaged in a righteous warfare with his society. In my view this is not an accurate picture of the relationship. I believe that there *is* a dualism of the individual and society, but that the dualism is not necessarily, nor even normally, one of conflict. The two are complementary and mutually supporting, and it seems idle to argue which is prior in order of time and therefore prior in order of natural right.

When we speak of "the individual," we are dealing with an analytic isolate, something abstracted from its context and held up for convenience of study or reference. For all Whitman's fine phrase, there is no "simple, separate person." The person is always a person within his society, and although it probably could never be proved which owes the other more, it is certain that the individual is indebted to society for many things which allow him to be an individual. He makes use of its institutions, its customs, usages, its settled preferences, and its means of communication in order to express himself in his own way; it is silly to think of being an individual alone in the big woods or at the North Pole. Thoreau's individualism showed itself in the rather long list of rejections of what his society presented and his continuing satire of its assumptions. This was his way of *using* what was offered; and we rejoice that his society was healthy enough to allow him to take the posture he chose to take and still "include" him.

It would seem to me false, therefore, to picture our task as always that of fighting the battle of the individual against any society. In a normal situation, the individual and his society are mutually sustaining in a complex, and while there will always be minor and incidental frictions, these will not be a prime feature of the relationship. We may derive some prescriptive guidance here from the principle that any sound whole respects its parts. It is made a whole by its parts; it is conscious of this, and it does not attempt to override them or distort them. And the part owes a loyalty to itself as well as to the whole; it must be itself in order that other *parts* may be themselves.

Following this line of analysis, I am disposed to accept the doctrine of Calhoun, which, roughly speaking, visualizes society as an organism made up of organic parts. If the organ as a whole is to function properly, the parts must be allowed to perform their offices. The head must not fight against the stomach or the arms try to take the place of the legs, and so on. This provides reason for saying that the parts have an inviolate character; they must be allowed to be what they are if the whole is to carry on its unitary function. Furthermore, there are some things the whole may not do without specific concurrence of the parts, so that in some matters the part has an absolute veto.

Taking this out of the language of metaphor and looking at society as a concrete thing, we can say that it has parts comprised of individuals and of groups and combinations of individuals emerging out of some common interest or feeling. These groups are con-

stituents of society, and the state has no right to disregard their needs and privileges, because in doing so
it would be working against its real end.

This principle contains the final rebuttal of totalitarianism. The totalitarian philosophy assumes that the
unit of the whole, or the totality, has all the rights and
that the constituent parts either have no rights or have
rights of an inferior order. On the premise of this doctrine, there is no such thing as oppression of a minority; if a minority stands in the way of something
willed by the totality (as it would work out, by a nu-
merical majority), it is condemned by that very fact,
and any means whatever may be used against it.

This can be a form of government, but it is not a
society in any true sense, for society is a system of
groupings which has as its purpose the expression of the
many needs, desires, and inclinations that are found in
a multitude of people, always of course with due prevention of invasions and excesses. The modern "mass"
looks with hatred upon any sign of the structuring of
society, perhaps just because its own desires are form-
less and irrational. As Hannah Arendt notes in her
exhaustive study of totalitarianism, "Masses are not
held together by a consciousness of common interest,
and they lack that specific class articulateness which
is expressed in determined, limited, and obtainable
goals."[6] The individual has the best chance in a society

---

[6] Hannah Arendt, *The Origins of Totalitarianism* (New York: Harcourt, Brace, 1951), p. 305.

which permits and even encourages many different centers of authority, influence, opinion, taste, and accomplishment. These things grow out of associations freely entered into by persons of common necessity, interest, or geographical habitat.

Something toward this end could be accomplished by drawing more sharply the line between government and society. The present tendency seems to be to dissolve society altogether and make everything government. But government is the *protector* of society, not something identical with it. It is only in the kind of spontaneous life that society lives that a person has a chance to be an individual and to express himself personally.

For that reason the widespread present efforts to exterminate the idea of class and independent association, and to override all forms of particularism, are to be firmly resisted. Some of them had their original impulse in idealism, real or perverted, but their effect would be to freeze our imaginative, cultural, and social life in a *rigor mortis* of bureaucratic domination.

Individuality and the General Will

Felix Morley

Felix Morley's distinguished career as a writer and educator has included being a Rhodes Scholar, editor of the Washington Post *(awarded a Pulitzer Prize for editorial writing), cofounder of the Washington newsletter,* Human Events, *and president of Haverford College. Among his books are* Freedom and Federalism *and* The Power in the People.

Politics today has become the art of reconciling two continuously antagonistic forces—that of Individualism and that of a General Will. The practice of this art is the more difficult because the characteristic of Individualism unquestionably has greater reality than the concept of a General Will. Yet the tendency of the times is to subordinate the fact of fundamental human differences to the fiction of identical human purposes. This disconcerting paradox merits examination.

The idea of a *Volunté Générale,* as first developed by Jean Jacques Rousseau two centuries ago, is not to be confused with instinct. Gregarious animals on occasion act as though controlled by a single cooperative purpose. So do migrating birds. The same spontaneous unanimity is apparent among human beings in periods of panic or passion. But Rousseau's theory of a general will, which is embedded in contemporary political thought, is wholly distinct from collective action of an instinctive, passionate, or capricious nature. It is the composite, at any given moment, of the presumably rational judgment of all mature and competent members of the group. The general will is therefore the whole of which the individual wills are parts. Without individuality, in other words, there could be no general will, not even theoretically.

Conversely, it must be admitted, there can be no individuality, except of a strictly physical nature, without some agreement which tends to give a certain validity to the concept of a general will. There had to be mutual agreement to discuss individuality and personality, for instance, before those subjects could be examined from different viewpoints by those composing even the present group. Our objective is to develop, or at least discover, a composite opinion on the subject of individuality. Whether or not that goal is reached it is certainly clear that we consider individuality incomplete unless it leads to, or at least tacitly accepts, some form of generalized agreement.

Undoubtedly the characteristics of individuality and personality can be found, and may to some extent be expressed, without a social setting. The primitive anchorite, isolated in a lonely cave, grubbing his own subsistence, is free from the modifications of individualism that society necessarily imposes. Man in the state of nature is indeed in a sense the only untrammeled individualist; the only independent and uncircumscribed personality. But what we really mean by individualism is the latitude of a person to choose for himself among the many fruits of a civilization in which he is an active participant. It is in practice impossible to cut oneself off from the disagreeable results of collective action, while continuing to benefit substantially from those regarded as pleasurable.

"Man is a political animal" who needs contact with his fellows—in work and play, spiritual as well as material—for self-fulfillment. On that point Aristotle said the last word. The prolonged helplessness of human infancy; man's unique ability to formulate and communicate abstract ideas; his desire as well as his need to cooperate with his fellows—these and other distinctive attributes combine to demand that association which of itself creates society. And I think we must all agree that social contact implies some form of that social contract on which Rousseau placed such great emphasis.

The social contract may of course be implicit rather than explicit. It may be as simple and elementary as the convention which allows the batter three strikes in a game of baseball. Or it may involve a constitutional division of power so complicated and refined that a Supreme Court must be established to make the determinations. The social contract, again, may be accepted willingly by citizens who have a voice in its application; or it may be enforced by terrorism on unwilling subjects. But these diversities, whether of importance or of acceptability, are all secondary to the fact that the social contract is a reality, and that no individual can with impunity ignore the terms made applicable to him.

Nevertheless, eminent political thinkers, especially in England, have since the French Revolution denied any validity to the theory of the social contract. Sir Frederick Pollock, for instance, calls it a "plastic fiction," while admitting sorrowfully that it "became one of the most successful and fatal of political impostures." Certainly it would be impossible to prove that groups of naked savages ever covenanted with each other to change the state of nature into an orderly political society. But such evidence is not necessary to validate this part of Rousseau's argument. There are many instances, in our own history, where men confronting primitive conditions individually accepted generalized rules and regulations for cooperative ends. The Mayflower Compact was one of these, and there were many others during the colonial period.

These social contracts, however, were of limited scope. The one drawn up by Roger Williams in 1636, for settlers in the new town of Providence, specified that it should apply "only in civil things." The novelty, and the danger, of Rousseau's *Contrat Social* lay in its all-inclusive, totalitarian nature. No aspect of human life was to be excluded from the control of that general will which Rousseau called the "essence" of the social contract. His key sentence is worthy of careful attention.

Chacun de nous met en commun sa personne et toute sa puissance sous la supreme direction de la volunté générale, et nous recevons en corps chaque membre comme partie indivisible du tout.

It is important to explore some of the consequences that follow inevitably from the assumption that everybody places "his person and all his power under the supreme direction of the general will." Clearly the thesis suggests, as Rousseau himself goes on to admit, that "whosoever refuses to obey the general will must in that instance be restrained by the body politic, which actually means that he is forced to be free." To many of us that still seems an impossible contradiction in terms—that one can be "forced to be free." But it is a conclusion that follows directly from Rousseau's premise.

In other words, a change in the character of self-determination is brought by the social contract. Through the agency of this contract man passes from the state of nature to the state of civilization. And in so doing he exchanges his natural liberty for what Rousseau calls civil liberty. Or, as I think we should put it in English, under the social contract man exchanges liberty, which is an individual attribute varying in its intensity and quality from person to person, for freedom, which is an artificial and external condition created, protected, and governed by social action.

Since our language is rich enough to possess the two

words, I think we should carefully observe the subtle but very real distinction between them. Liberty is to my mind an individualized spiritual aspiration, whereas freedom I regard as a generalized physical condition. As Rousseau suggests, many may enjoy freedom when the personal liberty of some is sharply restrained. And, conversely, one may keep the essence of personal liberty without freedom:

> Eternal Spirit of the chainless Mind,
> Brightest in dungeons, Liberty, thou art!

It is impossible to disagree with Rousseau's argument that society must have rules, and that those rules inevitably encroach on personality. If I am playing solitaire in the Castle of Chillon I am at liberty to cheat all I want and nobody else is affected thereby. But if my freedom is enlarged to permit me to play bridge with three fellow prisoners, I must observe the rules of the game. I must not slip myself an extra card in order to win, for if I do the losers will very properly protest, with a vehemence proportionate to the stakes involved. For the freedom of a social game I have surrendered the liberty I had at solitaire. And if you accept that homely illustration you have gone a long way towards admitting that the social contract, far from being "chaff and rags," as Burke called it, is an inevitable consequence of social contact.

American political thinkers, instead of vehemently denouncing the theory of the social contract, have been more inclined to set limits to its exploitation by political rulers. That is sensible. Where Rousseau can and should be criticized is for equating society and state, for setting up a mystical "general will" as sovereign power over both, and for then deceitfully asserting that the sovereign himself is bound, like his subjects, by this general will. It follows that the clear duty of those who believe in individualism is not to attack the unchallengeable part of the social contract, but to oppose its extension, through the now well-established myth of the general will, to every aspect of human life and thought. For while we can afford to give up liberty temporarily in a social game, we cannot afford to surrender it permanently to the state. This becomes more clear when we realize that the social contract operates on these two distinct levels, which are differentiated as society and state.

The distinction between the two was well defined and emphasized by Locke. His great influence on the Founding Fathers helps to explain why the difference between society and state is still more readily recognized by Americans than by Europeans. Essentially, society is the voluntary cooperative action of individuals in areas where the state is not concerned. But these areas are always subject to contraction if the state moves in to make cooperation compulsory. The rules of conduct laid down by society and those laid down by the state are in both cases binding and in both cases find their philosophic justification in the theory of social contract. The essential difference is that the rules laid down by the state are legalized, with physical force behind them, whereas the rules of society are primarily voluntarily agreements and are better described as conventions. He who violates a social convention is likely to be ostracized, or ex-communicated in the broad sense of the word. But he who violates a state law or edict is subject to impris-onment or even death.

On the moral scale, therefore, society is a superior type of organization, since its authority is based on individual agreement rather than on external coercion. Morally speaking, it is reactionary rather than pro-gressive whenever the state expands its authority at the expense of society. Social security, federal aid to edu-cation, unemployment insurance, governmental hand-outs, subsidies, and interventions of every kind, not least so-called mutual assistance to allied governments —all these, however dolled up in a specious humani-tarianism, are essentially reactionary measures, cal-culated to encroach on voluntary goodwill. Put arithmetically, the taxes I pay to support the expanding galaxy of governmental welfare measures diminish by just that much what I might contribute under the prompting of my own conscience through associations and in directions of my own choosing.

Rousseau's fatal achievement was not only to estab-lish the so-called general will as a political dogma, but also to convince his followers that it is somehow in every respect superior to the individual will, which in any conflict of opinion, in any sort of undertaking, must give way. Clearly this theory, integrated with coercion, involves a most cynical view of human nature. It implies that no man can be trusted to "live a godly, righteous, and sober life," no matter how heedfully he may incline to divine promptings. On the contrary, he must be constantly and subserviently attentive to the orders of Big Brother, who by some perverted miracle and political hocus-pocus has come to embody a general will. This, as Rousseau explained in very modern gobbledygook, may quite conceivably be unenlightened in any given circumstance, but nevertheless must not be questioned because *toujours droite*. So the successors to Stalin came to explain that they could not question that dictator when he was wrong because he was then interpreting a general will that is invariably right.

To understand how this pernicious doctrine ever took root one must, no matter how sketchily, locate the place of Rousseau in the long history of Western political thought. Aristotle certainly recognized the nature of the social contract. But he was very careful not to adulterate it with any nonsense about the general will. "From the hour of their birth," he wrote, "some are marked for subjection, others for rule." Moreover, "this duality originates in the constitution of the universe." On this point Aquinas later elaborated effectively.

With Christianity came a more humanitarian, *Vox Populi, Vox Dei,* conception of social contract. This broader conception became the charter of the *Civitas Dei,* from which slaves and barbarians are not excluded. So far as possible, political organization should also be in conformity with, or at least irradiated by, the teachings of Christ. Man-made law should conform to natural law, the principles of which are discoverable. And if this conformity is not always practical politics, then, at least the conduct of religious society should be free from control by the state. In Gibbon's opinion, it was the successful assertion of this prerogative that crumbled the Roman Empire.

With the Reformation, and the subsequent rapid rise of nationalism, political thinking inevitably lost some of these universal values, and despite the United Nations we have not yet found the formula to restore them. Machiavelli is a perhaps extreme example of the shift from idealistic consideration to eminently pragmatic statesmanship. For him the social contract was as mundane, as localized, and as limited a concept as it had been for Aristotle. Similarly, as seen by Hobbes, the ordering of the state was an essentially secular problem. Milton, among the Protestants, stands out in this period for his affirmation that: "Our liberty . . . is a blessing we have received from God Himself. It is what we are born to. To lay this down at Caesar's feet, which we derive not from him, which we are not beholden to him for, were an unworthy action, and a degrading of our very nature." That thought profoundly influenced the formation of American government.

But just before our Revolution came Rousseau, whose devastating influence was to displace both God and chivalry at a single push. His sovereign power—the general will—replaces divine authority with a hydraheaded monster not merely lacking in divine attributes, but also safeguarded against both *noblesse oblige* and any effective form of popular control. Yet this most arbitrary of all tyrannies is called democratic, and by the sheer emotional appeal of that dubious word brings a quasi-religious fervor to all who lack a more spiritual form of faith.

So it happened that the social contract ceased to be a self-denying ordinance and became instead a deceptively disguised instrument of oppression. We have not seen the end of it, for the "People's Democracies" of the Soviet world are the direct and logical outgrowth of Rousseau's conception of an unquestionable "general will." And the religious, but anti-Christian, fervor of modern communism owes much more of its proselytizing strength to Rousseau than to Marx.

If the theory of the general will had been voiced by itself, instead of being cleverly tied in with the valid conception of social contract, it would scarcely have survived, let alone prospered, as is the case. The major fallacy is too obvious. In the last analysis some ruler must interpret and promulgate what is assumed to be the general will. The more sacrosanct this popular desire, the more authoritarian must be the power of those entrusted with its realization. A single, unified popular will implies a single, unified governmental purpose to make the will effective. This is the road to dictatorship; not to what Americans mean when they speak of democracy.

Yet the theory of the general will can fairly be called democratic, and is indeed closely allied with democracy as we habitually use the soporific political term. Every adult who subscribes to the general will thereby acquires citizenship and every citizen enjoys an equal voice in any elections that are permitted. There is absolutely no discrimination—except against those who do not admit the premise. They, of course, are outlaws and worse than outlaws.

In rejecting the fiction of the general will these dissenters have also rejected the fact of the social contract and are therefore not merely noncitizens but also self-defined enemies of the community based upon the social contract. As at least potential traitors within the body politic they deserve, and will quite likely get, extermination. By the same token, however, adherence to the doctrine by somebody under another sovereignty makes him *concitoyen,* who should if possible be liberated from bondage. Burke, in his *Letters on a Regicide Peace,* estimated one-fifth of the influential people in England and Scotland to be "pure Jacobins," more loyal to revolutionary France than to their own country. Burke clearly saw that Rousseau's doctrines demanded

French action to liberate these British Jacobins from British rule.

This international aspect of Rousseau's democracy, taken over *in toto* by the Communists, has had a great appeal for idealists who are properly appalled by the narrowness and bigotry of flamboyant nationalism. A system which simultaneously promised emancipation at home and brotherhood in foreign relations could not fail to exert much influence, especially on youth. "Bliss was it in that dawn to be alive," enthused the youthful Wordsworth at the outbreak of the French Revolution, "but to be young was very Heaven!" Much the same rosy anticipation, in due course, was aroused by the "Ten Days That Shook the World" from Russia.

But the application of the general will, as distinct from its theory, must always lead to disillusion, both from the national and the international viewpoint. Rousseau would give all conforming citizens the vote and further insists that they should participate actively and continuously in politics. He did not observe that since the general will must come to a precise conclusion in any particular issue, and since this conclusion is by definition the only one then tenable, therefore any permanent division of the electorate along party lines becomes intolerable. The party that represents "The People" not only must dominate, but must extinguish all opposition to its program.

Moreover, the tendency toward a single-party system is strengthened by Rousseau's mistrust of parliamentary government. Like the Physiocrats before him, Rousseau disliked divided sovereignty. In place of an absolute monarch he enthrones the general will. In practice this means an equally omnipotent executive differing from the king only in being more demagogic and less assured of tenure. And to retain his supremacy against upstart rivals the spokesman of the general will must ruthlessly cut them down. The only valid political party is the one which gives the ruler unquestioning support.

So the implications of Rousseau's doctrine explain the bloody chaos in the later stages of the French Revolution, where no single man prior to Napoleon was able to hold the dictatorship long. *Mutatis mutandis,* it explains the abominations committed by Mussolini, by Hitler, and more intelligently by the Communists. In all of these cases the theory of the general will demanded the liquidation of any effective Parliament and the organization of a single fanatical party pledged to obey the fuehrer. The greater success of the single-party system in Russia would seem to be due partly to the better corporate discipline of the Communists and partly to their organization along international lines, which Rousseau himself would have strongly approved.

If the concept of the general will brings dictatorship in its train at home, the result in foreign relations is no less certainly a continuous threat of war. The nearest approach to unanimity in the thinking of a community is always found when an enemy is present or effectively portrayed, so that any absolute ruler is likely to bolster

his position by asserting that the security of the nation
is threatened. Beyond that, the spokesman of the general will can promote a crusading and missionizing
fervor among his people—to bring the truth to those
with less enlightened government. The leaders of this
messianic movement may, of course, formally renounce
all conquest or imperial rule, in keeping with their always humanitarian pronouncements. This was Robespierre's position early in the French Revolution, as it
was Lenin's when communism gained power in Russia.
But the dynamic is too strong for such self-denial, even
if sincere. Soon the armies move out—not to conquer
of course, but to "liberate." Thus international stability
is doubly disturbed—not only by the danger of aggres-
sion, but by the feeling that "preventive war" may be
the best way to resist a threat which is psychological as
well as physical in nature.

We can now see why Rousseau is rightly regarded
with abhorrence by all who realize that individuality
cannot prosper under the constant threat of total war.
While claiming to set men free, the ideas of this
warped genius have actually served to promote a
climate of slavery more threatening and more widespread than anything found in prerevolutionary France.
To attribute the monolithic state entirely to this one
neurotic personality would of course be overdrawn. As
well hold Hitler solely responsible for World War II.
But what we do find in the doctrines of Rousseau is the
evil seed from which, with cultivation, the brambles of

modern totalitarianism have spread. Voltaire summed it up very fairly, when he wrote to thank Rousseau for a presentation copy of the latter's *Discourse on Inequality.* "I have received your new book against the human race and thank you for it," said the great cynic. "Never was such cleverness used in the design of making us all stupid! One longs, in reading your book, to walk on all fours."

The inequality of men, this early study by Rousseau maintained, "is the first source of all evils." The wild assertion is elaborated and embroidered in *The Social Contract,* published in 1762. One might therefore conclude that the first of the "self-evident truths" proclaimed in our Declaration of Independence, fourteen years later—"that all men are created equal"—was inspired by Rousseau. But there is no confirmatory evidence. Jefferson does not appear to have been influenced by Rousseau until he went to France as minister, after our revolution but prior to the much more formidable upheaval there. Moreover, so far as the notes of Madison and others show, Rousseau's ideas were never once cited during the proceedings of the Constitutional Convention, whereas Montesquieu and Locke were both frequently quoted. The same is true of the *Federalist Papers.*

Since the very word "democracy," in the political sense of unfettered majority rule, was then anathema to most Americans, this is not surprising. Discussion of a hypothetical general will would have been academic, to say the least, when the immediate problem was the formation of a general government with any real power over the virtually independent states. A federal republic was all that was anticipated by the most determined early nationalists, like Alexander Hamilton and John Marshall. The protection of minorities *against* the majority was the inspiring and historically unique objective of the Founding Fathers. And if anyone at that time had suggested the desirability of a unified general will, to be defined and exercised throughout the states from the seat of central government, he would have been denounced more roundly even than was poor bumbling George III.

Nevertheless, it is a matter of record that the French apostles of Rousseau, if not the master himself, soon came into high favor in the United States. A good deal of the adulation showered on Citizen Genêt, when he arrived here as Minister of France three months after the guillotining of Louis XVI, was doubtless inspired by anti-British sentiment; some of it was probably just the indigenous American naiveté which would today give Bulganin and Khrushchev a thunderous welcome if they were allowed to come. Some of these Genêtics, if our biologists will pardon me, were due to Jefferson's decidedly francophile influence. But after all such discounts are made there is no doubt as to the underlying democratic surge, which burst forth in many places, and in many forms more dangerous than the poetic effusion from cultured Boston:

> See the bright flame arise,
> In yonder Eastern skies
> Spreading in veins.
> 'Tis pure Democracy
> Setting all Nations free,
> Melting their chains.

Far more serious, and worthy of recollection in these days of Communist cells, were the Jacobin Clubs which, with the open support of Genêt, sprang up in all our seacoast cities. When John Marshall went to France, on the famous X Y Z Mission, he was told by a deputy of Talleyrand, then Foreign Minister, that "the French party in America" would not tolerate any arrangement with the Directory—in settlement of just American claims—in any way burdensome to revolutionary France. The then extraordinary influence of Rousseau's disciples in the United States is given lengthy consideration by Senator Beveridge, in his famous biography of Marshall, and can there be readily reviewed.

But this American Jacobinism, significant though it was, ran contrary to the establishment of an American "general will." It worked against, rather than with, those who like John Marshall desired the establishment of a strong central government. To their last member the Jacobin Clubs over here supported Jefferson and opposed the Federalists. These clubs were the basis of Jefferson's Republican Party, which took that name partly to signify its sympathy with the revolutionary Republic of France. When Genêt was ousted, and the almost treasonable activities of the Jacobin Clubs were exposed, they logically changed their name to Democratic Clubs. There is certainly a lineal connection between the Jacobin Clubs of the seventeen-nineties, the later Democratic organizations like Tammany Hall, and the ADA of our own day. Rousseau, in short, is to be regarded as the real progenitor of modern democratic theory, in its "liberal" as well as its totalitarian form.

A paradox that demands interpretation is illustrated by the fact that the Jacobin Clubs, which served in France to concentrate political power, were in this country organized to resist a similar concentration. The political units that we call nations have varying cultural backgrounds and social customs. Consequently the theory of an immanent general will, when imposed on one country, will follow a somewhat different line from that which it would take in another country. In our own time the theory of the general will has been the starting point for the rise of Fascist Italy, Falangist Spain, Nazi Germany, and Communist Russia. In all of the first three, though with differences between them, the general will was made the tool of a relatively parochial nationalism, which of course was a strong factor in the French Revolution also. The role of Karl Marx was to emphasize that the international, communistic aspects of the French Revolution—the contributions of relatively forgotten men like Morelli, Babeuf, and Buonarroti—were really more vital than those of Mirabeau, Danton, or Robespierre. Of course Rousseau's incendiary ideas could most easily evolve within the confines of a national state, and through the control of a single government. In theory, however, they were thoroughly international. And we must realize that the establishment of a general will in a single powerful country is a sure preliminary to its attempted establishment for all mankind.

For the general will in practice necessarily becomes the will of the executive that has been able to seize power. And if it is to be internationalized this executive cannot permit the triumph of a rival general will in another country. Therefore the country that gets a running start in this direction, as did France in 1792, or Russia in 1917, must work against nationalism in other countries, although of course it may as a tactical matter temporarily promote nationalism in a colonial area. The vehicle for this subversive intrigue is the local revolutionary group, loyal to the alien idea and not to the institutions of the country where it operates. And the task of this group is fundamentally to promote the general will for which it works, and to oppose the development of any possibly hostile indigenous general will. Thus the Jacobin Clubs in this country did their by no means trivial best to oppose the growth of American nationalism at the time of the French Revolution, and thus the very similar Communist clubs, or "front" organizations, are today actively opposed to the development of American imperialism, which could so easily clash with that of Russia.

I have concentrated on the French Revolution, the enduring significance of which is all too little appreciated by Americans today, because it is so important for us to understand the long evolution of the present-day opposition to individualism. The fundamental threat, from the individualist viewpoint, is the *theory* of the general will. As Rousseau so clearly pointed out, this means conformity, not merely in the terms of a specific social contract which leaves personality inviolate and indeed protected, but also in the terms of an all-inclusive, overriding political obligation under which everything is owing to Caesar and nothing to God. In every field of life and thought loyalties are being increasingly secularized and within this narrowing compass man is now trapped as within that fiendish medieval instrument of torture—the Iron Maiden.

He struggles, naturally. Individuality and personality are far too deeply rooted to be exorcised by the mere wave of an egalitarian wand. But these struggles seem to be increasingly pitiful and futile, like those of an animal hopelessly trapped. The youngsters "rock 'n roll"—what horribly expressive terms—while their parents seek almost as feverishly for some sort of anodyne. If there is anything that can be called a general will it is the desire somehow to escape from the conditions that the figment of a general will imposes. But though we may rocket over our superhighways, in cars of ever-increasing speed, and power, and danger, still every road is overshadowed by the bomb. "In the event of an enemy attack this road will be closed."

And triggering the bomb is the grip of this absurdly named general will, becoming ever more generalized at the expense of helpless individuals. Some think they can oppose this concept, as now expressed from the Kremlin, by creating a contrary general will centralized in and directed from the White House. But this, of course, is the counsel of despair. It is the concept of the general will as such that is the enemy of individualism. If we are to cope with that enemy, before it overcomes us wholly, it is time to realize that the word democracy, used in a political sense, is simply Rousseau's monster garbed in currently fashionable dress. To say that the will of the national majority shall prevail, in every subject from the determination of profits and wages to the conduct of education, is merely to underwrite this dreadful fallacy. For the will of the majority is as specious as the general will from which it is derived. Even when intrinsically desirable it cannot in many fields be made effective. Of course every wage earner can be guaranteed ten thousand dollars a year, but what will those dollars then buy? Of course every youth can be given what may be called a college education, but what will be its content?

Men are created equal, in the sense that all have much the same basic needs, and in the sense that all are to be regarded as parties to whatever social contracts their communities may see fit to adopt. But at that point the line is drawn. To say that men deserve equal opportunity is tacitly to admit that with this opportunity they will become unequal. Some will push ahead while others will stay behind. "From the hour of their birth," to return to Aristotle, "some are marked out for subjection, others for rule." That biological fact can be concealed by sophistries, but cannot be successfully denied. Moreover, no system of government, least of all the alleged democracies, can prevent those who collect the taxes from dominating those who pay the taxes. The most that the ideal system of government can do is to insure that those who have the taxing power possess it only provisionally, and within clear-cut limits. Under such a system true individuality can flourish, because it is protected from the tyranny of the general will.

Where political power is concentrated and unlimited, as it must be under the theory of the general will, the unscrupulous are always likely to rise to the top. Those who recognize and cherish the infinite variety of human nature are by that fact alone estopped from issuing glib commands in the name of "the people." Here and there, for a brief period, a philosopher-king, a Marcus Aurelius, may emerge. But the odds are enormously against him, and in favor of the Neroes. It is of course bitterly ironical that starting from the assumption of human equality we move so easily to the conclusion of the one indispensable man. But that is merely another way of saying with Plato that the constant tendency of democracy is to slide into dictatorship.

For Americans, the picture is especially poignant, for in this country and in this country alone was it carefully planned to keep political power diffused, and therefore to promote the individual as well as the general welfare. The validity of the social contract part of Rousseau's political philosophy was admitted and indeed affirmed—by writing a Constitution in the name of the people which was eventually ratified, on the fulfilled understanding of a specific Bill of Rights, by all the states. But the theory of the general will was completely rejected and repudiated, not only by establishing a government with powers balanced between the executive, legislature and judiciary, as advocated by Montesquieu, but also by withholding all but enumerated powers from the central government as a whole. "The powers not delegated to the United States by the Constitution, nor prohibited by it to the States, are reserved to the States respectively, or to the people."

This system, still nominally in being, would seem to mean that the fiction of the general will, and its dreadful realization in the form of totalitarian democracy, could never take root in the United States. The majority will could be binding only in the field of delegated powers, and even there many specific restrictions were applied. "No bill of attainder or ex post facto law shall be passed"; "No money shall be drawn from the Treasury, but in consequence of appropriations made by law"; "Congress shall make no law respecting an establishment of religion, or prohibiting the free exercise thereof"; "No person . . . shall be compelled in any criminal case to be a witness against himself . . . nor shall private property be taken for public use, without just compensation."

A political system in which the majority will is so carefully hemmed about and circumscribed cannot with any accuracy be called a democracy and should never be called a democracy by those who take the oath of allegiance to the Constitution. Those who wish to destroy the republic, and build a unified totalitarian dictatorship on its ruins, will naturally want first to spread confusion as to what our form of government really is. Yet we find people of unquestionable patriotism asserting that our system is precisely what it seeks to avert.

Everybody who has convictions would of course like to see his convictions prevail. There are Roman Catholics who in their hearts would like to see their faith a state religion here, as it is in other countries. There are legislators who suggest, if they do not say openly, that Communists should not receive the protection of the Fifth Amendment. There are officials who argue that money should be withdrawn from the Treasury, for top-secret purposes, without prior appropriation. All that is only human, for very few minds are broad enough to see any problem in its full setting and it is always easy to believe that one's own opinion on any subject is more enlightened than that of the other fellow.

But let the dike of Constitutional guarantees be broken at one point, which you approve, and very soon the torrent will gush through elsewhere, very likely over the terrain that you yourself would most like to see protected. Give any viewpoint, no matter how worthy, a monopoly and others will very shortly claim the privilege. A free market, with truly competitive conditions, is as important in the field of political ideas as in that of commodities. And socialistic controls in the latter will very shortly be paralleled by socialistic controls in the former. Then, as that highly disillusioned Communist George Orwell informed us, we are in 1984. Then Soviet Russia has conquered us, whether or not the bomb is ever dropped.

The effects of two total wars have made the world all too safe for that totalitarian democracy which follows naturally, even inevitably, from Rousseau's doctrine of the general will. And the disease will not be eradicated until and unless its virulent germ is isolated and defined. In doing this individualists of every variety should make common cause, for whatever their individual bent it is menaced by the intolerable conclusion that, since men are all equal, the *summum bonum* is a dead level of standardized mediocrity. Doubtless that material level can be raised, under communism as well as under capitalism, to provide everybody with tiled bathrooms, electric gadgets, and chrome-plated automobiles. But men will never catch true happiness by herding like sheep down the blind alley of purely physical satisfactions.

It is not difficult to demonstrate that the doctrine of the general will underlies the belief that the majority is necessarily right, and that in political practice this belief means that democracy leads directly to dictatorship. The inevitability of that sequence, clearly foreseen by the men who wrote the Constitution of the United States, has been suggested here. What is not so apparent, but at least equally important, is the spiritual, as well as political, stultification to which the theory of the general will is sure to lead. By its innate hostility to individuality of every kind, this general will represses the personal contribution to better living into mass conformity. The result, for human beings, may be a very efficient, functional, and even architecturally beautiful anthill. But it can never have the qualities of the *Civitas Dei.*

As a political expedient, carefully safeguarded against tyrannical action, the device of majority rule has much to commend it. When the argument is over and the vote is taken, we can get on with the particular business, for better or worse. The danger comes when we convert the mere expedient of limited majority rule into the brazen idol that we call democracy; which Rousseau called the general will.

"Man is born free," complained this enemy of the human race, "yet everywhere he is in chains." After two centuries of experience with his remedial formula it is high time to reverse the aphorism. "Man is born in chains, yet under a government of limited and divided powers he may still be free."

Essay Five

Individuality vs. Equality

Helmut Schoeck

Born in Austria, Helmut Schoeck came to the United States in 1950 and became a naturalized citizen in 1956. After a postdoctoral fellowship at Yale, he taught sociology at Emory University. Since 1965 he has been director of the sociology institute at the University of Mainz in West Germany. He has contributed extensively to professional journals, and has written, translated or contributed to more than a dozen books. His most recent book in English was Envy: A Theory of Social Behavior.

To ask a sociologist for a contribution to a symposium on individuality is like asking a professional soldier to contribute to a symposium on pacifism. Sociology, or the science of society, for its very *raison d'être* had to ignore individuality, and has always done so with a vengeance.

Of course, this is studied ignorance for the sake of specific knowledge. Not a few sociologists, however, extend this epistemological ignorance of individuality to ontological absurdity, as I shall document later.

For the greater part of this paper I shall step outside of the field of sociology, in order to look at it critically.

As long as sociology treats individuals, or groups of individuals, as essentially equal units in the cognitive act, aimed at a specific sociological problem, it is legitimate. We could have no systematic knowledge in any field without epistemological acts of ruthless categorization, or shall we say, equalization. This does not harm the individual as such.

After all, five hundred paintings of five hundred individual beauties by great and individual artists hardly suffer simply because, for specific classification, they all come under the rubric of "portrait." Scientistic equalitarianism becomes a threat to individuality, both in social theory and in policy based thereon, only after confusing epistemological equality or identity with ontological equality.[1]

---

[1] It seems that sociologists have given up more and more what Lester F. Ward called pure sociology and have imbued their work with what he called applied sociology. As Ward defined it, "pure sociology is simply a scientific inquiry into the actual condition of society." We have now reached a point where pure sociologists, *e.g.*, Kingsley Davis, are attacked for the impediment of (presumably) applied sociology through their work in pure sociology. (Cf: the controversy between K. Davis and M. Tumin, *American Sociological Review,* August 1953.)

Many American sociologists today behave as if Ward's definition of applied sociology would have to cover all of their work. They are no longer aware of the difference between epistemological and ontological equality. I suspect that the borderline was rather thin even with Ward. He wrote: "Applied sociology differs from the other applied sciences in embracing all men instead of a few. Most of the philosophy which claims to be scientific, if it is not actually pessimistic in denying the power of man to ameliorate his condition, is at least oligocentric [This is an interesting term for the sociologist's professional crime of paying attention to individuality!] in concentrating all effort on a few of the supposed elite of mankind and ignoring or despising the great mass that have not proved their inherent superiority . . . it may be said here *that from the standpoint of applied sociology all men are really equal"* (italics added). Lester F. Ward,

A long time ago, man discovered that to have a science of any area of observable data we must treat phenomena as *if* they were identical. But this is valid only for the purposes of the particular science of a particular field.

Taking things as equal—mentally—in order to investigate them as units in a series, in order to study their structural similarities and causal relationships, should not be confused with treating these things as equal ontologically. But many social scientists have done exactly this to their units of study, which are men. Here, they are quite unlike the physician who keeps, as a rule, prognostic and diagnostic statistics apart from his clinical approach to unique individuals. Nor does the physician try to remake the individual according to a statistical average.

In the statistics of the demographer, even of a cultural demographer, the individuals of a given population are, by and large, naked numbers only. A similar position is held by the consumer in the economist's tables. Otherwise there could be neither demography nor economics. It does not follow, however, that—as wartime or socialist rationing laws and coupons always tend to do—consumers must be treated, in their indi-

---

Applied Sociology, 1906, pp. 4f. Karl Mannheim approvingly discussed the assumption of "ontological equality of men" in the social sciences in his essay, "The Democratization of Culture," *Essays on the Sociology of Culture*, 1956.

vidual act of consuming, as if they were equal units. This peculiar notion, inherent in centralistic economies, leads to such actions as the criminal prosecution and punishment of two consumers who innocently exchange their ration-card coupons, *e.g.*, a nonsmoker trading his tobacco coupons for the chocolate coupons of a smoker who doesn't care for candy. Both in Britain and in Germany this self-assertion of individuality in the act of consuming was classified as a criminal action during World War II.

A pragmatic conceptual equalization of unique phenomena ought not to become an ontological equalization when we deal with human beings.

This confusion of epistemological equality of human beings with ontologically normative equality, leads some sociologists and anthropologists to thinking that they are engaged in scientific work when actually they may do little more than ask people: "Don't you worry about your inequality?" or "Why don't you demand equality with everyone else?"

These *social* scientists, I am afraid, are on par with the *physical* anthropologist who might inquire whether the short members of our species resent the advantages of tall ones, or ask the bald males whether or not they feel insecure in the presence of those who boast a full mane. What would be thought of medical doctors who would ask the crippled, the blind, the toothless, whether they see the difference between their own bodies and those of others?

Many a teenager's ego suffers a worse and more lasting blow on the day he finds he must wear spectacles than on the day he discovers his school is restricted to his range of IQ. Shall we, therefore, compel the entire population to wear spectacles, so that the deficient will not feel inferior? It may yet come to this. The welfare state principle of "giving" all citizens equal old-age pensions, irrespective of need, is based on exactly this motive. To remove the sting of inequality from the provision of public support, all must be made to accept it, no matter how wasteful this system.

The present confusion in social science is even greater than so far indicated. While pushing epistemological "equalitarianism" into the realm of human ontology, the very same sociologists, it seems, do not dare make all of *epistemological* equality that could be gained by applying this principle consistently and vigorously.

By this complaint I mean the following. A great deal of contemporary research in social sciences, especially in sociology and social psychology, is probably a fantastic duplication of effort. Survey after survey, small group study after small group study, is being carried out. But few are the scholars who dare draw a line after the nth small group study and declare that from here on each repetitive study will simply duplicate what we already know. In other words, these scholars do not see fit to proceed along the assumption of a reasonable identity of human behavior under given circumstances, though this assumption would allow them to get off the merry-go-round of pure induction.

Our social scientists tend to postulate a strange and unprovable equality of human nature and human potentialities when it comes to basing social (welfare) policy on social science. This is the confusion of epistemological with ontological equality. Yet the same scientists, their practical equalitarianism notwithstanding, refuse to assume enough of identity of situational human behavior to get out of the rut of endless research duplication.

Professor George C. Homans of Harvard is certainly one of the more moderate among the empiricists. Yet my point here comes out quite strikingly in an article of his in the *American Sociological Review* of December 1954. He says: "I shall describe briefly a study of the ten girl 'cash posters' in an accounting division of a certain company, and it formed part of a study of the division as a whole, which I carried on from December 1949 through April 1950. Since it deals with only one group and that group had only ten members, it can hardly hope to establish general hypotheses about small group behavior. Several such studies, made with comparable methods, might hope to do so, and they would provide the indispensable background to more macroscopic studies of worker behavior, made by questionnaires. But by itself the present one can only be called a case study of the relations between repetitive work, individual behavior, and social organization in a clerical group."

If this is all Dr. Homans has learned after spending several hours daily for several months with ten girls in one room, nobody but the Ford Foundation can help him. At least he should be able to generalize about all females of our species in small working groups. But if our social scientists show such reluctance to generalize and predict where it would seem so reasonable, how can we trust their assertion that the basic equality of humans warrants equalitarian social policies?

Individuality, rightly understood, is incompatible with the ideal of "equality of opportunity."

Harold J. Laski, in his book *The American Democracy* (1948, p. 718), declared:

> . . . No one has yet been able to make a successful frontal attack on the idea of equality. From the time of John Adams . . . social theorists in America have sought ways and means of undermining its place in the American tradition . . . in the end, the strength of the egalitarian tradition has been profound enough to leave it as the central thread in the American tradition.

Laski might well have quoted from letters Justice Holmes wrote him between 1927 and 1930:

> I have no respect for the passion for equality, which seems to me merely idealizing envy. . . . Some kind of despotism is at the bottom of the seeking for change. . . .

Nonetheless do I repudiate the passion for equality as un-philosophical and as with most of those who entertain it a disguise for less noble feelings. . . . I don't know anything about the right of every man to an equal share on chances. . . . As to the equality business I don't see any ground for your aspirations in the prospect of improved economic conditions for the many. . . . What I can see more clearly is the desire to get rid of a disagreeable contrast in position and public esteem—a desire for which I have little respect.[2]

The sort of equality Laski advocated never prevailed in all spheres of life in this country. For one thing, "equality" has too many different meanings. This probably has reduced its political effectiveness. As Daniel J. Boorstin wrote recently, in his *The Genius of American Politics* (p. 176):

. . . Take our concept of equality, which many have called the central American value. No sooner does one describe a subject like this and try to separate it for study, than one finds it diffusing and evaporating into the general atmosphere. "Equality," what does it mean? In the United States it has been taken for a fact and an ideal, a moral imperative and a sociological datum, a legal principle and a social norm.

The United States became the economically most prosperous nation precisely because over here equalitarianism in practical life rarely meant equality of con-

---

[2] Holmes-Laski Letters, edited by Mark DeWolfe Howe, 2 volumes, 1953, pp. 942, 1089, 1101, and 1272. The correspondence contains many additional critical remarks by Justice Holmes on "the equality business." They can be easily found through the excellent index.

ditions. Foreign socialist critics are aware of this. In 1949, Lord Lindsay of Birker observed that democratic equality in America was "thought of as the right of anyone to become unequal. It is an equal right to inequality." Apparently our more emotional spokesmen of equality nowadays more and more ignore or simply fail to comprehend this. Often they seem to press for legislation which *at the same time* would compel movement toward equality of condition *and* equality of opportunity to become unequal in the process. Such a confusion could only create chaos.

Our professional equalitarians are not as unchallenged as Mr. Laski suggested. In current scholarly literature, in social as well as biological sciences, there is an increasing opposition to equality as a legitimate goal and norm. Outstanding scholars express grave misgivings about equalitarianism and what attempts to enforce it may do to a society. When isolated findings and thoughts are integrated they will show that individuals as individuals do not want to live in a truly equalitarian society.

It is true, however, that to a greater or lesser degree in all societies the life of the individual is always in a delicate balance between individual self-assertion and fearful submission to the imaginary collective. Probably that has always been the case. In preliterate as well as in complex societies the individual is subject to control by other individuals due to the construction of a mythical entity: the "whole society."

If reformer A would say to invidious individual B, "Desist from conspicuous consumption because it irks me," he would neither impress B, nor gather much support from indifferent members of the society. But if the reformer succeeds in making people believe first in such an entity as "society," he can subsequently graft his own wishes of social control on that anonymous body. The theologian John Bennett well expresses this type of thinking when he writes that: "Economic activities should be undertaken for the sake of the whole society, and economic power should be under the control of the whole society."

With very few exceptions, which were years of economic growth and innovation, the periods of human history have seen individuals labor under the controlling myth of a "whole society." So we tend to forget that mankind's emergence from stereotyped and stagnating ways of life, on low subsistence, has exclusively depended on the emergence of independent and enterprising individuals, in various fields of endeavor, who had enough resistance to escape from social controls which were usually imposed in the name and interest of "the whole society" or nation.

The rise and ever wider impact of social science undoubtedly has helped to recreate an intellectual climate in which men are apt to forget that "society" cannot make demands on individuals that are justified by supra-individual knowledge. In *Individualism Reconsidered,* David Riesman recently wrote: "Social

Science . . . led us to the fallacy that, since all men have their being in culture and as a result of culture, they owe a debt to that culture which even a lifetime of altruism could not repay . . . since we arise in society, it is assumed with a ferocious determinism that we can never transcend it . . . [such concepts] . . . destroy that margin of freedom which gives life its savor and its endless possibility for advance."

How can individuals break through the social controls of "society"? The concept of good and bad luck is, apparently, one cultural definition for that purpose. Some cultures (tribes) lack the notion of good and bad luck (for instance, the Navaho Indians). In such societies it is extremely difficult for individuals to enjoy the fruits of differential faculties, insights, motives, and, of course, of good fortune alone.

On the basis of an extensive study of this particular problem I am inclined to say that, among other things, in a given culture it is precisely the lack of a strongly embedded notion of good and bad luck which keeps societies on the lowest possible level of subsistence. Economic growth, a rising standard of living, acceptance of innovation in agriculture and sanitation, all call for the concepts of good and bad luck. They are a form of internalized social control on aggressive resentment which functions both in the successful and in the failures.

We should not assume a dichotomy between the

favored few and multitude of failures. In the sense that there is only one President of the United States, one of GM, and one of Harvard, virtually all of us may consider our lives only a partial success. The concept of good and bad luck serves a function for every member of a given culture. It not only bridges the gap between aspiration and achievement but also makes vertical mobility and individual innovation psychologically tolerable. Even those already fairly high up in the socio-economic structure need that belief. Very few indeed will ever attain so philosophical or religious a position that they can place their lives in tolerable perspective without the concept of good and bad luck. A mere extension of so-called equality of opportunity cannot assure perfectly adjusted people who regard each other as complete equals. Somewhat belatedly in Great Britain this is dawning even on radical proponents for equalitarian social change.

In so "progressive" a journal as *The New Statesman and Nation* (August 14, 1954), for instance, there was examination of the question whether or not maximization of equality of educational opportunity may not be even more dysfunctional than some old-fashioned relative injustice. A social survey, *Social Mobility in Britain,* edited by D. V. Glass of the London School of Economics, aimed at discovering the extent to which people move up or down the social ladder, or remain stationary upon it. Part of the investigation consisted in obtaining ten thousand life histories revealing mobility between the generations, and the relationship between this mobility and such factors as marriage and education. One of the most striking implications, which recurs constantly throughout the book, is that within a couple of generations there may be "perfect mobility" except for the few attending fee-paying schools—if there are any left. "But what will happen then? What will equal opportunity really mean?" asks the reviewer in *The New Statesman and Nation*. Professor Glass suggests this possibility:

> The working out of the Act through the three-fold system of grammar, technical and modern secondary schools will by no means minimize the disadvantages of the new unstable relationships between successive generations. On the contrary, the more efficient the selection procedure, the more evident these disadvantages are likely to become. Outside of the public schools, it will be the grammar schools which will furnish the new *elite,* an *elite* apparently much less assailable because it is selected for "measured intelligence." The selection process will tend to reinforce the prestige of occupations already high in social status and to divide the population into streams which many may come to regard, indeed already regard, as distinct as sheep and goats. Not to have been to a grammar school will be a more serious disqualification than in the past, when social inequality in the educational system was known to exist. And the feeling of resentment may be more rather than less acute just because the individual concerned realizes that there is some validity in the selection process which has kept him out of a grammar school. In this respect, apparent justice may be more difficult to bear than injustice.

Thus, we see that any approximation to "equality of opportunity" (a really complete one is impossible) is probably more disruptive of human relations than the inequalities of the past and present. Professor Glass warns that lack of adequate social research did not prevent the passage of the 1944 Education Act, which could destroy the democratic society which paradoxically produced it.

Why did we not have such research? And why, currently in America, is there more research designed to find out how to produce an equalitarian society than there is research asking whether such a society is possible? It should be a warning that even *The New Statesman and Nation* is forced to ask whether the desire to produce a society of equals will not "simply end in one which is just as rigidly stratified on an IQ basis as it was once by birth."

It seems that only the existence of unequal external opportunities makes it possible for the unsuccessful individual to live with himself. As long as unequal chances are known to exist, failure can be blamed on external conditions, rightly or wrongly. But how can the individual think well of himself, how can he face relatives and friends, if IQ tests and personality factors alone have determined his place in society? Social scientists, pushing men into unrealistic aspirations to, and beliefs in, irrational "equal opportunities" may actually produce the frustrated human beings whom they like to explain as victims of the present social system.

It will probably be granted that prestige, power, beauty, love, and a host of other goods and values cannot be "redistributed." But what about "economic equality," frequently demanded as a step toward providing more equal distribution of the less tangible values? Possibly the claim for economic equality is as irrational as are the others.

To date no one has found a way to measure it. Carrying economic equality by law to any conceivable approximation, let alone to perfection, would wreck any known type of human society. Can we even aim at *relative* economic equality, as a vague goal to guide our policies? Recently, two American authors have tried to make a case for it. Robert A. Dahl and Charles E. Lindblom devote more than five hundred pages to outlining a socioeconomic system moving ever closer to equality.[3] First they call "equality" a key value on which everybody ought to agree. Later they attack reliance on incentives because "it might easily produce such inequality as to demoralize a population rather than develop desirable incentives."

These authors propose "income distribution toward more equality [as] desirable on three grounds: for sub-

---

[3] Robert A. Dahl and Charles E. Lindblom, *Politics, Economics, and Welfare,* 1953.

jective equality, for political equality and stability, and as an investment in resources."[4] However, toward the end, they write: "Few people in the United States would have the temerity to advocate inequality and imbalance, even though they might mean by these words precisely what the advocates of national bargaining mean by equality and balance."[5]

In short, Americans are so awed by the mere word "equality" that meaningful discussion is no longer possible. Little wonder that Dahl and Lindblom offer continuously contradictory statements, for example: "Of course political equality is never attained in the real world." And then: "Our own preference for political equality is based upon a psychological want and a strategic calculation that may well be applicable to general equality. But unfortunately, general equality is almost impossible to define."

They admit that in a highly *inegalitarian* society individuals are likely to feel better (as was suggested by the above mentioned study in Great Britain). They think correctly (p. 48) that "class identification limits the guilt felt by an upper class toward an inferior and the envy felt by an inferior class toward upper classes." Why then are the authors dissatisfied with a condition common to every known human society? Dahl and Lindblom quite candidly answer: "One cannot be at

---

[4] *Ibid.*, p. 138.
[5] *Ibid.*, p. 506.

all sure that he would be among the elite to whom the advantages of inequality would accrue."[6]

At this point, a quotation from Bernard Berenson may be illuminating:

> Unfortunately, jealousy is not confined to sex. It will be hard to get the better of it in persons who resent every inequality that does not suit their heart's desire. . . . Resentment is unhappily at the bottom of more social discontent than economical difficulties. When these last are overcome, as in the course of time they may be, inequality of physical make-up, of mental and moral gifts, will remain and fester in many natures.[7]

The motive of jealousy in Dahl and Lindblom's equalitarianism is suggested by their claim that "income goals cannot be met by a larger national income without further equalization." Why? "Almost no one in the United States, for example, lacks income for sufficient dental care. Yet large numbers of people are convinced they cannot afford it. . . . The explanation is, of course, that social standards and pressures compel them to turn their expenditures in other directions."[8]

Will Dahl and Lindblom solve the dilemma? On page 147 they say that: "No one can 'solve' the problem of the best distribution of income." Yet on page

---

[6] *Ibid.,* p. 48.
[7] *Rumor and Reflection,* paragraph selected as a memorable citation in the *New York Times* Book Review Section.
[8] Dahl and Lindblom, *op. cit.,* p. 146.

158 they assert: "Given time for recruitment of new generations of management . . . an adequate supply of vigorous, imaginative management can be had through much smaller differentials in money income than those now prevailing." Also: "If certain occupations could not be filled, it would be those in which the work was undesirable or the status low. Hence differentials needed for occupational mobility would be reversed. Today's low paid jobs would be highly paid."

This book by Dahl and Lindblom is a recent and voluminous pleading for equalitarian policies. The dubiousness of this sort of economic and political writing is finally indicated in the authors' conclusion: "Not only are we—and, as we believe, others—unable to demonstrate the 'ultimate rightness' of these values [equality, 'rational social action,' *i.e.,* a planned economy], but we cannot even demonstrate conclusively that the characteristics of man and social organization make these values attainable enough to serve as relevant social goals."[9]

One of the most dangerous tendencies in contemporary thought is the attempt to drive a wedge between maintenance of individuality and private property. The latter always must include the freedom to lose as well as to gain. An inconsistency of so-called progressives is that they advocate freedom to hurt oneself for chil-

---

[9] *Ibid.,* p. 517.

dren, but deplore that freedom for adults in economic life.

Sometimes, collectivists define individualism almost exclusively as the freedom to be Bohemian:

> Individualism and individuality: A final ambiguity in the problem of individualism remains to be faced. Usually, "individualism" is used in American discourse, particularly in political argument, to refer to economic endeavor and enterprise. It connotes striving in some self-reliant and relatively unfettered (particularly by government) way for achievement and success, in short, the acquisitive urge. This notion is not identical with what we may call "individuality"—the right to be "one's self," to develop one's own individual personality as far as possible according to one's own values and tastes, to be different, to be a nonconformist, to dissent from orthodoxy if one thinks it necessary, in short, the right to diversity.[10]

Private property is inextricably linked to human individuality. We can find no *evolutionary* principle in man's attitude toward private property and its linkage to his individuality, privacy, and concept of personality. Some writers point to primitive property sharing, but for every preliterate form of communal property there are offsetting instances of pronounced individualism in regard to property. To infer from a particular custom of indefinite lending, or actual sharing, that it is somehow natural to man to have a communal atti-

---

[10] *The American Social System* by S. A. Queen, and others, 1956, p. 459.

tude toward property is about as realistic as to conclude that American office mates are Communists because they share dictionaries, newspapers, and paper clips. Perhaps just because we have shifted our concern with property to larger and more important things, we can afford to be lax toward communal use of office stamps or garden tools.

Primitive man, however, extends his personality especially into small items of property about which we would hardly worry. Parry reported from the Lakher in India "that the most dangerous thing to leave in another's house is a closed basket containing . . . money. When the owner comes to fetch [his basket] . . . he must give the owner of the house a fowl to sacrifice to avert the danger of threatening him."

Why? We have a casual visitor who forgets his briefcase in our home. He is neither a Soviet diplomat, nor a physicist in an atomic plant, but an ordinary fellow working on his own income tax return and carrying his notes for this worthy purpose. When he returns to pick up his briefcase, there will be an uneasy moment. We will wonder whether or not he thinks we did or did not pry. Either way, it will be embarrassing to both parties. Among the Lakher, the forgetful visitor has to pay damages for having inflicted this emotional pain on his host.

This shows how well recognized the sphere of privacy can be even among very simple people. It also suggests that no matter how crude their economy, such people view each other not as equals but as very distinct individuals. In fact, among many simple tribes, each member is thought to possess the faculty of impressing his unique individuality or personality, like a seal, on every item of property, on any discovered fishing spot, in short, on anything he may deem valuable to him. He leaves his sign and the thing or place is protected from all fellow tribesmen. We no longer have such magical powers, except that our children may on occasion protect a piece of cake from their siblings by putting some of their saliva on it.

In short, it would seem that the prime notions of privacy, individuality, and personality are essentially independent of the level of civilization and complexity of social organization attained.

The so-called acquisitive urge is practically universal among men. Complete lack of property is for man, at all times and under all known cultural conditions, an extreme situation. Probably, the universal consciousness of private property is linked to the universality of sexual jealousy. Personal property and gain are essential supports and shields of the basic family unit. To expect man to surrender his acquisitive urge is to expect him to give up his possessive attitude toward wife and children. It would seem that those American theologians whose collectivism induces them to pick from anthropology what they think supports their view on the unrelatedness of private property to human nature, have not only falsified anthropological data but also by implication attack the universality of the family. It is significant that the only truly equalitarian communities in our present world, certain villages in Israel, operate under a system that keeps children from the day of birth until age eighteen in communal nursing homes with the express purpose of extirpating the notion of private property.

We should ask whether equalitarianism in contemporary mass democracies will be self-limiting, whether it will come to a rest after reasonable additional economic stabilizations? I doubt it.

Not long ago, a candidate for the doctor's degree, filled with passion for equality, submitted the first draft of a doctoral dissertation, parts of which were concerned with cultural engineering in the United States. Among other things, the young man seriously proposed a supreme cultural planner. One of the tasks of this bureaucrat would be to arrange for social conditions assuring every American "equal sensory experiences of esthetic objects."

Somehow, it was unbearable for this student to live his invidious life of a genuine connoisseur in a society where a great many, as he suspected, cannot differentiate between art and trash. In other words, he felt as guilty for his unique (individual) sensory and cognitive esthetic experiences as he did with regard to his family fortune.

This encounter showed me with terrifying clarity that the threat to individuality in any equalitarian system is always infinite and never self-limiting. That young man, devoted to the religion of equality, had come to propose a scheme which would doom nearly all the values and artistic possibilities for which he stood.

In principle, this problem arose in a controversy between T. S. Eliot and Harold J. Laski almost ten years ago. Laski contended that in his society of equals the lowliest laborer would grasp all of Beethoven, which leaves open to question why he should go on digging ditches instead of teaching music. No matter how ridiculous these ideas may seem, there is no reason to take lightly the actuality and danger of aggressive envy on the part of that population segment which cannot, or will not, experience the esthetic values held by a minority.

I shall never forget a conversation I overheard in Germany during the Third Reich. It was after a performance of Puccini's *La Bohème* at the Munich State Opera. The house had been well filled with common people, and as I was walking home I heard two young women, in front of me, have this exchange:

The first: "Did you understand that? Did you have any fun listening to that crazy music and singing?"

The second: "No. Not at all. You know, I really hated those people next to us who looked as if they enjoyed that sort of thing. It must be great to be like them."

The first: "Don't worry. They don't understand it either. They just pretend. I am sure of that."

These two factory girls, or perhaps typists, had been told by national-socialist indoctrination that all Germans must have an equal share of the cultural heritage (proffered free of charge). The only way to reconcile their own deficiencies with the doctrine of equality in the *Volksgemeinschaft* was to doubt the differential experience of the others.

Hitler, probably in compensation for his own early failure, had become an equalitarian dictator of art. Individual deviation was anathema. The whole German people was to be molded into an audience of equals, compelled to enjoy, or at least attend, a limited repertoire of approved esthetic forms. Consequently, any expression of esthetic criticism had to cease also since it would have been an insult to the whole society of "equal connoisseurs." To some extent, Hitler had achieved what our young liberal American graduate student so hopefully desired. There simply is no single field where equalitarianism will not lead into blunt totalitarianism.

Now, it could be that some German connoisseur, afflicted with similar social cowardice or "conscience," sitting next to the factory girl sent to the opera on a free ticket (the cost deducted from her wage), felt less guilty for his own individual cultural experience just because he rubbed elbows with her. But, as my observation would suggest, he was not thus safeguarded from the envy and hatred of one with a more limited range.

Alexis de Tocqueville again and again exposed the dangers of progressive equalitarianism to the American democracy. Attacking it, he explained that the almost irrepressible emotion of envy is stimulated under democratic conditions, especially if the gifted few in a society are committed to delude the "common man" with false notions about his inherent capabilities. If people are equal politically, then how can they endure their remaining inequalities? Pondering on this dilemma, Tocqueville clearly foresaw the new despotism, the rule of mediocrity, the demand for "less for all."

T. S. Eliot's play *The Confidential Clerk* in my view is a wonderful satire about the goal of *equality of opportunity*. Actually, the goal is unattainable. Yet such an admission would be untenable for present-day intellectuals bound by the unwritten rules of modern social science research. When I read Brooks Atkinson's review in the *New York Times* I began to understand the special reason why this play irked most drama and literary critics in America.

The theme of *The Confidential Clerk* can be found in the following lines:

> If you haven't the strength to impose your own terms
> Upon life, you must accept the terms it offers you.

Now let's see how these lines fared under fire of Brooks Atkinson's equalitarian attack. After opening night, he wrote:

> *The Confidential Clerk* has to do with inherited characteristics and a man's duty to accept his place in the world. . . . It takes a lot of patience and study to discover what Mr. Eliot is saying by indirection, he looks so bland and mild on the surface. And if, by chance, he is saying that everyone should be satisfied with his lot in life, it is possible that many of us do not want to hear it.

Apparently Mr. Atkinson did not. A few days later he wrote about the new play:

> [I take] the liberty of concluding that Mr. Eliot means to say: we should be resigned to our lot in life, we should accept the terms life imposes on us and "adapt ourselves to the wish that is granted." This is a rather chilling thought. It eliminates struggle and rebellion. It encourages docility. Despite his benignity and modesty there is a chilling side to Mr. Eliot's acceptance of established authority.

Not at all. Eliot said, "If you haven't the strength to impose your own terms . . ." Obviously, he felt that only in such case ought we to accept what is in store for us. What Eliot ridicules is the dogma that a parental monetary situation and equal educational opportunities are the major factors making for success or failure in a man's life. Eliot emphasizes the primary power of hereditary factors, which are uniquely and unevenly scattered among mankind.

Everything seems so simple as long as we assume that men are born with equal endowments of intelligence and emotional stability. Some time ago, I heard a Yale professor urge his graduate students to accept the necessity of a welfare state "because all people are born with about the same innate chances for success in life." This would suggest that only the income of the father is the deciding factor in whether child A is to become President of Yale or whether child B is to end his career as a bum. T. S. Eliot's sociology appears closer to reality.

B. Kaghan, the accidentally lost son of the lady in Eliot's play—despite the most unfavorable circumstances in his early life—is portrayed as a rising man of means, who, nobody in the play seems to doubt, will end up as a rich and influential alderman of London. On the other hand, Colby actually is the son of lower-class parents with inferior faculties. His mother smuggled him into the educational opportunities of a rich man's son. This woman symbolizes the socialist who exploits the sentimental and unfounded guilt feeling of the wealthy for doing *en bloc* what Colby's mother did with her own son. But the moment Colby learns of his real origin, his aspirations shrink. He shows full contentment with his modest lot, freely chosen by himself. That kind of contentment is a state which equalitarian social scientists must ignore and deny.

Finally, what is "Equality of opportunity"?

Is it possible to distribute property in such a way that say, at age eighteen, the sons of a university president and the sons of a dock worker would have the same chances in life, as far as economic and social status are concerned? Of course not, as a modicum of psychological insight tells.

To be the son of a well-educated family means to have a certain number of implicit educational opportunities; also it means to *know* educated and professionally advanced people. This is one of the reasons why, again and again, collectivists sneer at the institution of the family. It simply does not tie in with the ideal of equality.

In order to give every individual the same chance, and nobody a better one, the government—for one thing—would have to prevent A from having a better credit rating than B. Otherwise good luck, close study of legal loopholes, initiative, risk-taking, and persistence will make rich men even under today's taxes. But credit ratings are also linked to individual character traits.

All this leads to a frightening conclusion. *Literal* equality of opportunity could be accomplished only by eradicating the memories and personality traits of each individual at a given age. If you could thereby remake men into identical atoms of society, the equalitarian might at last be satisfied. And it was exactly this naive mechanistic view of man in the eighteenth century from which the ideal of equality emerged.

Perhaps, if the proponents of equality by "leveling" continue to have their way, an obligatory electroshock treatment plus lobotomy for every young person reaching a certain age will become standard procedure. Today, this is still mere satire.

In J. B. Priestley's recent play, *Take the Fool Away,* in a utopia somewhat similar to Orwell's *1984,* the authorities subject individualists to lobotomy. These "lobos" are then harmless robots, working for the state and laughing only when induced to do so by a special injection. But it would not be the first satire to evolve into grim reality. The agents are ready.

Last year I had a talk with the director of teacher education in one of our universities. The jovial gentleman confided his greatest worry to me: "You know, our graduates, after four years of indoctrination in our program, go out from here with pretty much the same attitudes they had when they came as freshmen. I really think we ought to get permission to electroshock them."

Individuality and Its Significance in Human Life

Roger J. Williams

Roger J. Williams was born in 1893 in Octacumund, India, and received his Ph.D. in biochemistry from the University of Chicago. From 1939 to 1971 he was professor of chemistry, and since 1971 professor emeritus, at the University of Texas. He also served as director of the Clayton Foundation Biochemical Institute from 1941 to 1963, and has been a resident research scientist there since 1971. A past president of the American Chemical Society, he is the author of numerous books on chemistry, nutrition and vitamins. Among his books concerned with individuality are The Human Frontier, Free and Unequal, Biochemical Individuality *and* You Are Extraordinary.

B efore embarking upon a discussion of individuality, it seems desirable to delineate just what is meant by the term. To the writer, in the present context, it means: *the possession of distinctiveness by members of the human family.* Yet consultation of five leading dictionaries fails to reveal a single definition or quotation which clearly embodies this idea. All are in substantial agreement with the complete definition as given in *Webster's New World Dictionary of the American Language* (1951) which is short enough to quote *in toto:* "1. the sum of the characteristics or qualities that set one person or thing apart from others; individual character; 2. the condition of existing as an individual; separate existence; oneness; 3. a single person or thing; individual; 4. (obs.) indivisibility; inseparability."

The first of these definitions is the most germane, but certainly does not encompass the meaning which it is desired to convey in the title of this discussion. A parallel inadequacy would be to define gravitation as *the force that attracts one body to another*. Gravitation is more than this; it is the force that attracts all bodies to each other.

Similarly, individuality is more than that which resides in a person; it resides in every person. This fact—which probably no one will deny—is, in the writer's opinion, one of the prime facts in human history and one of the prime factors in human relations. The failure of the lexicographers to recognize this meaning of the word is a testimony to the neglect from which the subject of our discussion has sorely suffered. The proposed definition does not include any doctrine, policy, theory, or practice relating to individuals; these may be covered by the word *individualism*. Neither does it carry any implication *a priori* as to the importance of individuality, how pronounced it is or how it shall be managed or interpreted. Some of these points will be touched upon in this essay.

What facts relating to the possession of distinctiveness by members of the human family can we assemble and how do these bear on human problems and their solution? This is an incomparably large question.

Before approaching it directly, it seems well to dispel certain misconceptions which may stand in the way of considering fairly the material which is to be presented. Because the writer is a scientist he does not spell science with a capital S. He has learned, he believes, "the great lesson of humility which science teaches us, that we can never be omnipotent or om-

niscient," and that "man is not and never will be the
god before whom he must bow down." There are many
questions which human minds are apparently not
equipped to answer. The great Einstein developed
remarkable new insights into how gravitation operates,
but I am told on good authority that he had not the
vaguest glimmering as to *why* it operates.

So it should not be concluded that I am confident all
questions can be answered on a mechanistic basis and
that there is no room in my thinking for human wills
and aspirations or for anything other than a deterministic
outcome. If this were my attitude, I would not participate in this discussion. Actually, the handiwork
exhibited in the biochemical realm is in its way as
impressive as that seen in the heavens, and becoming
acquainted with some minute portions of this realm
may increase rather than decrease one's reverence
and awe.

Concerning the ubiquity of individuality we can, I
believe, accept without danger of contradiction the
categorical statement that every human individual
(even in the case of identical twins) is distinctive and
different. This will be so generally accepted that the
statement may well be regarded as trite.

The question of the ways in which distinctiveness is
exhibited, however, and the extent to which different-
ness exists, is one on which we will need to spend some
time and thought, because it is crucial to the whole
discussion. One may accept and give lip service to the
idea of distinctiveness—all the time being ignorant

about the character of the differences and perhaps even assuming that they are inconsequential. If they are indeed inconsequential, then our whole discussion belongs in the same category. We shall therefore address ourselves to the question: What differences exist and how consequential are they?

The ways in which people differ from one another may be grouped under four headings: (1) anatomical, (2) physiological, (3) biochemical, and (4) psychological. Never in the history of science and human thought, to the best of my knowledge, has anyone ever made a serious attempt to look at these differences specifically or to gain an overall view of them. In this relatively short discussion it will not be possible to do more than present briefly a few of the outstanding findings, including some references for those who wish to explore the subject farther.

While it has been common in the past for students of anatomy (in medical schools for example) to learn little about normal variations, such variations are abundantly present and cannot safely be regarded as trivial.

Although the textbook picture of the human stomach, for example, is well stereotyped, there are enormous variations in shape and about a sixfold variation in size.[1] The position of the lowest portion of the stom-

---

[1] Barry J. Anson, *Atlas of Human Anatomy* (Philadelphia and London: W. B. Saunders Co., 1951).

ach relative to the sternum or breastbone, in normal individuals, may vary in height through a range of about eight inches. It is no wonder on the basis of these facts alone that people exhibit individuality in their eating.

Livers, likewise, vary greatly in shape and position and at least threefold in size. The length of the small intestine is commonly said to be twenty-two feet, but even when only a few autopsy specimens were measured recently, they were found to vary in men and women from eleven feet to twenty-five feet nine inches.[2] The relative position of the transverse colon varies in its position in the visceral cavity. In some individuals it is about twelve inches lower than in others. The forms of the pelvic colons may be classified into nine different types, and it becomes immediately evident that a high degree of individuality with respect to problems of elimination would be expected on the basis of these anatomical differences alone.

Musculature throughout the body is far from uniform in different individuals. As an instance, there are eleven patterns involving the extensor muscle of the index finger alone! These differences in muscular patterns are present throughout the body and are associated with bone and tendon differences. There are, for example, eight patterns of the extensor tendons on the back of

---

[2] Betty Underhill, *British Medical Journal,* November 19, 1955, p. 1243.

the hand. It is no accident that people exhibit individuality in their signatures and that even small children exhibit a high degree of individuality in their motor skills. Muscular and other differences are also associated with the fact that each individual has a highly characteristic breathing pattern, has a distinctive heart action (as shown by blood pressure tracings and electrocardiograms), and exhibits individuality in his manner of performing any gross muscular activity, such as walking, running, throwing, rowing, etc., and that individual capabilities and distinctiveness exist for delicate operations such as those involved in tapping out telegraphic messages, watchmaking, surgery, or even following the profession of pickpocket.

The blood vessel patterns in the bodies of actual individuals do not follow any single textbook picture. The major arteries arising from the aortic arch may be from two to four in number, and when there are four, they are not necessarily the same four in different individuals. The size of the carotid artery which carries blood to the brain varies greatly from individual to individual—as do all other vessels which carry blood to specific localities. These variations are superimposed upon those existing in the heart. The pumping capacities of the hearts of young men—even though they are healthy and normal—vary over more than a threefold range.[3]

---

[3] G. C. Ring and others, *Journal of Applied Physiology*, 5, 1952, pp. 99–110.

Endocrine glands vary widely from individual to individual. Thyroid glands, for example, may vary in weight, among normals, from nine to fifty grams,[4] the parathyroids (two to twelve in number) vary in weight from fifty to three hundred milligrams. The testes in normal males weigh from ten to forty-five grams; the ovaries in females vary in weight from two to ten grams and contain at birth from thirty thousand to four hundred thousand ova. The pineal glands weigh from fifty to four hundred milligrams, and pancreas glands contain from two hundred thousand to two million five hundred thousand islets of Langerhans.[5] The adrenal cortices of different individuals are said to vary about tenfold in thickness.[6] It should be emphasized that the values given above are "normal" ones. Other values outside the above ranges are not infrequently encountered, but they are regarded as abnormal. Certainly no one could survey the endocrine field and conclude that the differences among individuals are trivial.

Our entire nervous system is subject to the same wide variation, which is not only anatomic but physiological as well. The patterns of the nerve trunks are distinctive. There are, for example, eight distinct types of patterns

---

[4] Arthur Grollman, *Essentials of Endocrinology,* 2nd ed. (Philadelphia: J. B. Lippincott Co., 1947).

[5] Gregory Pincus and Kenneth V. Thimann, eds., *The Hormones* (New York: Academic Press, 1948), I.

[6] Max A. Goldzieher, *The Endocrine Glands* (New York and London: D. Appleton-Century Co., 1939).

of the facial nerve, differing from each other almost as much as do river systems on different continents, each type possessed by from 5 to 22 percent of people. The lower point at which the spinal cord terminates in the spinal column in different individuals varies by about three vertebrae; the point of entrance of different nerves varies similarly. Most people have two splanchnic nerves, but some have three. Some do not have direct pyramidal nerve tracts in the spinal cord. In a recent study of recurrent laryngeal nerves in one hundred cadavers it was found that of the two hundred nerves present, 57 percent entered the larynx without branching whereas 43 percent were divided-trunk nerves with from two to six branches.[7] This same kind of variation —probably even greater—is exhibited with respect to the number and distribution of the numerous types of nerve endings. If we are considered to be "bundles of nerves," each of us is a very different kind of bundle, and the anatomical variations are accompanied by variations in physiological performance.

The individuality in anatomy is also very evident in our brains. K. S. Lashley, in *Psychological Reviews* (1947), states: "The brain is extremely variable in every character that has been subjected to measurement." At another point, he says: "Even the limited

---

[7] William H. Rustad, *Journal of Clinical Endocrinology and Metabolism,* 14, 1954, pp. 87–96.

evidence at hand . . . shows that individuals start life with brains differing enormously in structure; unlike in number, size, and arrangement of neurons as well as in grosser features." While there is no need to overemphasize the importance of our brains, anatomically speaking, or to oversimplify their functions, it will be generally agreed that they do have something to do with thinking processes. When brains are so very different from one another, we should not be surprised that individuality in thinking is the rule rather than the exception.

A most important point in connection with these anatomical variations is the fact that no individual has "about an average" anatomical makeup. To emphasize this let us consider ten anatomical items which can be rated quantitatively (as, for example, size of organ or gland). If we assume that these anatomical variations are independent of each other (which is permissible for the purposes of this illustration), then the chance that an individual picked at random will be in the middle 50 percent of the range with respect to one item is 1 in 2. However, the chance that he will be in the middle 50 percent with respect to *all ten* items is only 1 in 1,024! Real people exhibit individuality and in a sense are always exceptional people.

Physiological individuality is exhibited to a marked degree no matter what area we consider. In that of the senses, for example—seeing, hearing, tasting, smelling, the sense of touch, etc.—striking evidence of individuality can be found wherever we look. Let us consider the sense of taste.

Creatine, an organic compound prominent in muscle, is bitter and biting to some and absolutely tasteless to others. Phenylthiocarbamide is extremely bitter to the majority of individuals, but to a minority (from zero up to 40 percent, depending on the ethnic group)[8] it is quite tasteless. Arthur L. Fox has found that sodium benzoate tastes bitter, sour, sweet, salty, or has no taste, depending on the individual tested. Some individuals find saccharin to have two thousand times the sweetening effect of sugar; to others, it is only thirty-two times as effective as a sweetening agent.[9] For some, quinine is two hundred fifty-six times as bitter as cascara; for others, it is only twice as bitter. To 15 percent of people mannose elicited no taste response, to 20 percent is was sweet only, to 10 percent it was bitter only, and to the rest it was sweet and bitter in succession. Curt P. Richter has found children who could not detect the sweetness of a 20 percent sugar solution. In our laboratories we have found that tenfold and even hundredfold variations in the taste sensitivities of different individuals for such common substances as

[8] William C. Boyd, *Genetics and the Races of Man* (Boston: Little, Brown & Company, 1950).

[9] A. F. Blakeslee, *Science,* 81, 504–7 (1935), and *Proceedings of the National Academy of Sciences USA,* 21, 1935, pp. 78–83, 84–90.

sugar, salt, potassium chloride, and hydrochloric acid are commonplace.

Rather than delve farther into the area of the senses we may be content with a quotation from the late Albert Blakeslee, who conducted many studies along this line: "Evidence is thus given . . . that different people live in different worlds as far as their sensory reactions are concerned."

Whether we consider heart action, brain waves, circulation, breathing, the endocrine functions, the blood, temperature regulation, or a multitude of other facets of physiology, the story is the same—abundant evidence of individuality involving differences of great magnitude. The *enormous* variations observed by Kinsey are ample evidence of wide degree of individuality in the area of sex physiology.

Let us now turn to the area of my particular competence, biochemistry, and look very briefly at some of the evidences of individuality which may be found there.[10] These evidences may be grouped under five headings:

Compositional differences. A relatively large amount of information is available regarding blood composition, because repeated individual samples can be collected and analyzed. The existence of blood

---

[10] Roger J. Williams, *Biochemical Individuality* (New York: John Wiley and Sons, 1956). See also *University of Texas Publication,* May 1, 1951, No. 5109.

groups has been recognized for over fifty years, and it is now well established that individuals are distinctive with respect to the content of immune substances in their blood. The protein-bound iodine of the blood varies from individual to individual over at least a five-fold to tenfold range, and remains relatively constant for each individual. The bloods of different individuals vary in their content of various types of lipides; and in the case of cholesterol, lipide phosphorus, and titrated fatty acids, at least, the individual differences are persistent.

The digestive juices of different individuals vary in composition. The hydrochloric acid content of gastric juice of healthy adult individuals collected under exactly comparable conditions varies from 0.0 to 66.0 milliequivalents per liter; the latter value is twice the mean value. Some normal individuals have at least four hundred times as much pepsin in their gastric juice as others.

We are different even in our bones, as is shown by a recent study by Dr. Pauline Berry Mack in which it was found that the bones of normal young men of the same age vary in density over a 5.7-fold range! These densities were determined by careful X-ray measurement of the *os calcis* (heel bone).

Eyzymatic differences. Most of the chemical reactions taking place within our bodies are catalyzed by specific enzymes which are produced in our bodies from the food we eat. The potentialities for producing these numerous enzymes clearly reside in the genes which we get from our forebears.

Repeated samples of blood from the same individuals have been studied sufficiently to know the content with respect to four enzymes: alkaline phosphatase, arginase (corpuscles), choline esterase, and amylase. In the case of each of these, every individual tends to maintain a characteristic level, and the variation between individuals is from threefold to fiftyfold. Other enzyme levels, in general, probably would show distinctiveness also, if the necessary data were collected. Two individuals of the same height and weight may have basal metabolisms (summation of the oxygen consumption of every organ and tissue) which are about the same, but the details of the metabolism of each may be very different indeed from those of the other. Some specific chemical reactions may be taking place ten times as fast in one individual as in the other. That this is actually so is shown by an experiment in which the utilization of the amino acid D-phenylalanine was repeatedly measured in the same individuals. Of the four individuals tested, one utilized it to the extent of 94 percent, one 61 percent, one 31 percent, and one 3 percent. Even in this very small group there was a thirtyfold spread with respect to the one item.

Excretion patterns. Extended investigations in our laboratories, involving the use of the newer tools of analysis, have shown conclusively that each individual exhibits a distinctive urinary excretion pattern. These studies help to clear up the question of how a blood-hound can tell one individual from another. Our body chemistries are manifestly different one from another, and individuality is everywhere in evidence.

Nutritional differences. Two clear-cut cases may be cited in which it has been shown that there is a wide spread in individual nutritional needs for specific substances. A careful study was made of nineteen healthy young men, to determine in each case how much calcium intake was required in order for the individual to be in calcium equilibrium—that is, free from calcium loss. At one extreme was an individual who needed only 3.52 milligrams per kilogram of body weight; at the other extreme, the corresponding requirement was for 16.16 milligrams.[11] This 4.5-fold range was observed when a small group of nineteen young men were studied; if a large group of men and women were to be investigated in this regard, the range would probably be much larger.

Another clear-cut case is that of the amino acid threonine. William C. Rose found for a small group of healthy young men that the range of needs was from 0.3 to 0.5 gram per day. For a small group of women the corresponding needs were more recently found to be from 0.1 to 0.3 gram. For men and women taken together, the range is fivefold, and if the groups of

---

[11] F. R. Steggerda and H. M. Mitchell, *Journal of Nutrition,* 31, 1946, pp. 407–22.

individuals had been larger, the range would doubtless have been larger.

Differences in pharmacological reactions to chemicals and drugs. Whenever a chemical or a drug has a physiological or pharmacological effect on an individual, it does so because of an *interaction* between the chemical or drug and some body constituents of the individual. If the *same* drug or chemical affects two people differently, it must be because the body chemistry of the two individuals is not the same. The individuality in response is shown in an experiment in which the minimal concentrations of mercuric chloride required to cause skin irritation in a series of thirty-five individuals were determined.[12] One responded to a concentration of 1 part per 100,000, another to 3 parts per 100,000, 5 more to 10 parts, 11 more to 30 parts, 13 more to 100 parts, and 4 failed to respond even at this level. This more than hundredfold variation in a relatively small group of thirty-five is indicative of large differences in microscopic anatomy and body chemistry.

A recent study was made on twenty-nine healthy young men involving the effects of morphine injection.[13] Saline controls were used. The drug caused

---

[12] See A. J. Clark, *The Mode of Action of Drugs on Cells* (London: Edward Arnold & Co., 1933), p. 107.

[13] Jane E. Denton and Henry K. Beecher, *Journal of the American Medical Association,* 141, 1949, pp. 1050–57, 1146–53.

nausea in 18, sleep in 16, drunkenness in 9, dizziness in 13, itching in 9, and indistinct speech in 7, more than one of these effects being apparent in some of the subjects. It is well known that this drug excites an occasional individual instead of causing depression and that some individuals, unlike others, are prone to become addicts.

Finally, let us consider the physiological effects of alcohol. Nagle[14] found that 0.25 ounce of alcohol had the same effect on certain individuals as did ten times the amount on others. Jetter[15] found in a study of one thousand individuals, using objective tests, that 10.5 percent were intoxicated when the alcohol blood level was 0.05 percent, whereas 6.7 percent were *sober* when the alcohol blood level was eight times this high, or 0.4 percent. Later a study of eight hundred more individuals was completed, confirming the earlier observations. To look for evidences of biochemical individuality is to find them.

The study of individuality in the area of physiology and biochemistry is in its very early infancy. Some of the basic facts upon which its foundations rest— namely, that genes in a sense beget enzymes (as well as morphological features) and that enzyme efficiencies vary through the operation of partial genetic blocks

---

[14] John M. Nagle, *Journal of Allergy,* 10, 1939, pp. 179–81.
[15] W. W. Jetter, *American Journal of Medical Sciences,* 196, 1938, p. 475.

—are still very new to science. Every recognized treatise in the fields of biochemistry, physiology, pharmacology, and physiological psychology is written on the assumption that normal man, the prototype of all humanity, is the primary if not the exclusive object of study—he, above all, is to be fathomed and understood. With this basic philosophy I am in strong disagreement.

In the area of psychology the existence of individuality has long been recognized, and a number of books have been written on the psychology of individual differences. Such study has received, in my opinion, a tiny fraction of the attention that it deserves, and the findings are often pitifully inadequate. Too often such study has been thought of as a wart or blemish on the face of the developing *science* of psychology. The idea that there are two kinds of people, those with normal and those with abnormal psychology, is valid only in the crudest and most superficial sense.

There are two incontrovertible lines of evidence which indicate that every individual has a distinctive mind-pattern, that is, a pattern or profile of mental capabilities. One is found in the numerous cases of individuals who have at best mediocre abilities along the conventional lines covered in schoolwork, and yet excel —some of them to practically unbelievable extents— in some special way: mental arithmetic, memorization, mechanical ability, artistic ability, musical ability. Such individuals have been sometimes designated as "idiot-savants," an unfortunate designation which sets them aside as freaks, to be considered quite apart from all other human beings. This appraisal is not fair, however, because these individuals are in a real sense caricatures, and observing them can tell us much about ourselves.

José Capablanca was an example of an individual who had moderate intellectual attainments in most respects but extraordinary abilities along lines necessary for playing chess. He won the first chess game he ever played—with an experienced enthusiast—at the age of five. On one occasion, in the course of seven hours he played one hundred and three experts simultaneously and won all but one game—a draw. Could anyone doubt that he had a distinctive profile of mental abilities?

Albert Einstein was doubtless the great mathematical genius of his time. His mental powers in some other directions were, however, not impressive. When a small child, he was very slow to learn to talk—even at nine years of age his speech was halting and slow. As a scholar he was evidently not apt in language as exemplified by the fact that even though he came to the United States, several of his books were written in German and translated by others into English. If Einstein's linguistic abilities had been on a par with his mathematical abilities, he probably would have been intrigued by language and would have written freely in languages other than his mother tongue. There is strong evidence, on the basis of his early school record, that he had a very definite and uneven pattern of mental abilities.

It is my opinion that every individual exhibits a distinctive profile of native abilities but that most of us have less prominent peaks than do the Capablancas or Einsteins. That this is so is indicated by the studies of primary mental abilities by Thurstone.[16] Such abilities as arithmetical facility, rote memory, word familiarity, and space perception, are possessed *unequally* by typical individuals. Individuals can be trained in any of these, but if two individuals who are far apart initially are trained the same length of time they will be farther apart after training than they were before training. Psychologists have great difficulty—when they make the attempt—in separating and identifying what are truly primary mental abilities, but the existence of distinctive patterns of mental abilities can hardly be doubted. I recently went through the results of tests on about two hundred prospective college freshmen who had been examined for "verbal" and "mathematical" proficiency. In about 30 percent of them, there was a wide disparity between the results of the two types of tests, each of which was given twice

---

[16] L. L. Thurstone, *Primary Mental Abilities* (Chicago: University of Chicago Press, 1938), and L. L. Thurstone, "Primary Mental Abilities," in *Centennial,* Collected Papers Presented at the Centennial Celebration, Washington, D.C., September 13–17, 1948 (American Association for the Advancement of Science, 1950), pp. 61–66.

and averaged. In accordance with this crude and very limited measure, about 70 percent showed no very distinctive pattern. If the measurements were refined and detailed, all would doubtless have exhibited patterns.

Even in this short discussion of individuality in mental abilities, it should be pointed out that evidence in this area is enormously strengthened by that in the areas of anatomy, physiology, and biochemistry, where the evidence is more direct and less subject to interpretation. On the basis of the biochemical, physiological, and anatomical evidence, the existence of psychological individuality would be presumed to exist even if there were no direct evidence.

Having reviewed briefly the question of what differences exist among human beings and how great these differences are, we may well turn our attention to the question of *how these differences arise*.

This brings us to the historic nature-nurture controversy, which in the minds of biologists has been completely resolved so far as its general outlines are concerned. No organism or attribute of an organism exists except as a result of interplay between heredity and environment. The importance of hereditary variation (individuality) cannot be minimized because without it evolution would be impossible.

It is no secret, however, that the trend of thinking in the field of the social sciences is environmentalistic. Even geneticists have leaned over backward in this regard and have seemed unwilling to stand up to the sociologists. This attitude is based in part on an attempt to escape from determinism—"if heredity is involved there is nothing we can do about it." Actually, following the dictates of pure reason and leaving out the possibility of an individual being able to direct his own life, environmentalism leads to determinism just as inevitably as does hereditarianism. The mechanist can say that no organism ever has control over its environment; every "movement into a new environment" is merely the result of tropisms and conditioned reflexes —responses to the old environment.

If, on the other hand, we possess some capability of ordering our own lives—and this is the crucial point— then neither heredity nor environment, nor any combination of them, leaves us helpless and without choice. We cannot escape determinism by shifting to environmentalism. This is intrinsically just as deterministic as hereditarianism. The only escape is the possession of an endowment which makes possible some direction of one's own life.

Let us assume, for the moment at least, that human beings have this directive capability. How then can they exercise choice in the face of a distinctive (and even fixed) heredity? If, for example, I have been endowed by heredity with the makings of an excellent singing voice, I have many choices. I can cultivate it as an amateur or as a professional; I can try for opera, for jazz singing, for yodeling, or whatnot; I can even (though this is unlikely) forget it. If I am endowed with some special ingenuity, I can use it on the one hand to perpetrate hoaxes, or in more "constructive" ways. If I am physically attractive and have the attributes which would make it easy for me to seduce young girls, again I have choices—among which is that of marrying early and being a "respectable" husband.

I emphasize this point of alternatives because of the complete absurdity, in my opinion, of the widespread idea: "If it's hereditary, we can do nothing about it." Even if we have unquestionable hereditary diseases, we are not, and will not in the future, be without recourse. When nature provides me with a defective pair of eyes, I may buy spectacles to correct the difficulty. If they do not work perfectly, I cultivate activities which do not require the type of vision that is beyond me. If I am born with diabetic tendencies, I learn to use insulin effectively—and so on and on.

Among the myriad of potentialities with which every individual is born, there still are an infinite number of possibilities of development—*provided this ability to order one's own life exists.*

If we can accept this point of view, we are in a position to look directly and without too much bias, at the question of how much heredity contributes to our individuality and to our individual lives.

I cannot take the space here to amplify my opinion that heredity contributes *enormously* to making us *individuals,* anatomically, physiologically, biochemically, and psychologically. This does not deny the indispensable interplay of environment. Indeed it is important to emphasize that environmental influences—particularly nutrition—are capable of doing *far more* than is commonly supposed, to contribute to the solution of genetically rooted human problems.

Environmentalism, however, is indefensible in the light of modern knowledge. So is the position of the hereditarian. The genecotarian position, which recognizes the interplay between genetic and ecological factors, is the only point of view which can stand up in the light of our modern knowledge of biology. Furthermore, it is essential that we develop expert genecotarians—those who are expert in adjusting the environment to the distinctive genetic needs of human individuals. One cannot be expert in this area unless he is versed both in human genetics and in human ecology (environments).

Having considered some of the facts of individuality, and how individuality arises, we are ready for a summary treatment of the key question, namely: *What significance do these differences and the resulting individuality have in human life?*

In widespread areas of human interest individuality is of the utmost importance. It is indispensable for *evolution*—this is a well recognized fact of biology.

Politically, individuality is fundamental. If we did not possess individuality we would all have the same tastes in eating, drinking, reading, art, music, religion, and all other pursuits and would willingly submit to regimentation and censorship in all matters. If our distinctiveness involves mere trivialities, then our love of liberty and our desire to make our own decisions are trivial also, as I have suggested in my book, *Free and Unequal.* Government by the people is justified only because we all have distinctive patterns of mentality and by pooling our faculties we can hope to come out with better answers than if we heed one man (a dictator) who has his own mental pattern and may be very incompetent in some respects. Effective pooling of our faculties is not easy. *Socially,* individuality is just as indispensable. Without individual differences, in makeup and in function, a free society could not exist.

In *medicine,* recognition of the scope and importance of individuality is indispensable to progress, and holds tremendous potentialities for the future. Up to now there has been too much lip service to individuality; far too little development of expertness with respect to the problems it presents. Failure to recognize the importance of individuality is probably responsible for development of much of the *mental disease* which afflicts us in this modern day. Everyone likes to be appreciated and loved. Many suffer from inconsiderate treatment because they will not and cannot fit into the mold prepared by society for them. The successful treatment of mental disease likewise must take into account the individuality (in all respects) of the individual treated.

Crime very often has its roots in the failure to recognize the existing extreme individuality and to find activities (jobs) that each individual can do and like.

Family relations could be greatly improved by additional knowledge about individuality. Wives, husbands, and children suffer and produce suffering in others when they are forced into a mold or an attempt is made to "make them over."

Race problems flourish on lack of appreciation of individuality and of interracial differences. In this area we desperately need "more light and less heat."

In the field of *education,* the recognition of each child's individuality (as it really exists) can hardly fail to produce a revolution in attitude if not in practice. Each child should begin, even in nursery school, to learn about himself and his fellows, to respect their individuality, and pave the way for decisions as to how he will order his own life.

Philosophy cannot fail to be affected by a better appreciation of the far-reaching character of individuality. Grandiose generalizations about the nature of man will have to be scrutinized. Individuality explains in part why there are so many philosophies, and so many questions that philosophers individually think important. Philosophies have been generated by men with *many* different patterns of mind.

In the field of *fine arts,* individuality plays a tremendous role. The creative artists show marked individuality, and the appreciators likewise. We cannot all be taught to like the same things because we are not built alike. We can possibly avoid being angry with one another because of differences of taste.

Individuality is basic to the development of *religious belief* or disbelief. William James' classic *Varieties of Religious Experience* would not have been written were people not constituted very differently mentally and emotionally from one another.

Indeed, it seems that an unrealistic and false view of the Christian doctrine of the brotherhood of man has served as a strong deterrent to the recognition of human differences (and the individuality which they denote), in spite of the fact that the worth of individuals is basic in all the teachings of Jesus.

Essay Seven

The Historian and
the Individual

James C. Malin

James C. Malin received his Ph.D. at the University of Kansas and taught there beginning in 1921, becoming professor emeritus in 1963. He is a past president of the Agricultural History Society and a fellow of the American Association for the Advancement of Science. His books include The Grassland of North America, Essays on Historiography, On the Nature of History *and* The Contriving Brain and the Skillful Hand.

The twentieth century is an age dedicated to science, so-called, which in the United States is in fact mostly technology. In such a cultural environment the historian finds his position peculiarly difficult. He comes to realize that it is all but impossible to make himself understood and to defend his professional role as expounder of the unique. Science deals with generalization about data arranged in groups by the process of classification, according to selected criteria. The search for laws is the function of science. The application of such laws to supposedly useful purposes is technology. Thus functionalism, which has always received emphasis in the practical United States, became the watchword of the twentieth century.

History, on the other hand, is unique in an absolute sense. Each person is biologically unique, and each fact or situation is the product of unique causation in space and time—a particular space and a particular time.

The study of history is intellectual enterprise, the object of which is to reconstruct the record of historical reality to the closest approximation reasonably possible. As the materials of history and their combinations are unique, occurring at particular times and places—not just anywhere—there can be no laws in history, nor recurring patterns, predictability, or functionalism. In an absolute sense there can be only one possible reconstruction of historical reality. Historical method must be as unique as the past reality it seeks to reconstruct. The nearest approximation of accurate reconstruction of the past is attained by dealing with the past as a whole, though not of course with the whole of the past. History is irreconcilable with either science in general or social science in particular. History is *sui generis*.

History is concerned with space, time, and change. It is concerned also with the unique person, with the unique event, and with their combinations. A differentiation must be recognized, however, as to what is possible in historical study for time prior to and after the advent of written records. Both periods have a history, but convention has rather generally and arbitrarily limited the term *history* to the time since the advent of the written record. This restriction, without clearly defined reasons, has had an unfortunate effect on both areas and has caused misunderstanding about their interrelations. The justification for differentiation which is valid concerns the critical problem of the role of the individual item of data as distinguished from the role of groups of data in history and science—the distinction between the nature of history and of the sciences.

Historical actuality is unique and irreversible. Prior to the appearance of man upon the scene it was independent of man. Since the advent of man, he has participated in historical actuality, and his unique records were added to the classes of records left by preman processes. These man-records are roughly of two kinds, unwritten and written. The record expressed in written language introduced into the situation for the first time the possibility of identification in the record of unique individuals and of recognition of them as persons distinguishable from the groups within which they had previously been submerged—not in life, where their individuality was recognized, but in the documentation of that role of singularity.

Convention has differentiated history recorded in written documents from everything prior to writing and has called it history, as separate from what the same convention calls prehistory. The only validity such distinctions possess is that the subdivision is a matter of convenience, making intelligence effective. An unfortunate effect, however, has been that the essential historical actuality is obscured, or lost to sight, just because of the peculiarities of the documents. *Both* history and prehistory as so defined dealt with people, unique individuals, in spite of their inability in the earlier time of leaving a written record of that individuality.

The nature of the documentary records of history imposes the necessity of different tools and procedures for reading and interpreting them. The purely geological record requires one set of specializations; the biological record adds another; the different earth sciences require still others; the prewriting man-records make further additions necessary. And the written man-record, with its potential of isolation and identification of the individual, introduces a wholly new order of magnitude into the problem of reconstruction of historical actuality, its records, and their interpretation. It is important to emphasize that the addition of the written record did not limit the historian to that new class of documentation, although, unfortunately, such limitation has been too largely accepted.

As participant in these conventions about periodization and fragmentation of history as comprehensively described, the historical profession permitted itself to be placed in a false position. To be sure, written-record history is man-centered because men wrote the documents. But men also made the artifacts of the archeologist, and geological history is no less history because pre-man-geological records were made without the participation of man. Furthermore, geological history still continues with man as a participant in the making of the record. Man as a species may become extinct, and in his stead a wholly unpredictable being may arise to operate upon this earth. Would man's sojourn upon the earth, together with its written record, be ruled out then by definition as geological history, as prehistory, or, as not-history?

In view of these considerations, it is important that perspective about history and about its nature be preserved. It is imperative to intellectual integrity about history, even about that infinitesimally small segment which relates to the sojourn of man on earth as a language-writing being, to focus upon the verbalization of the problem by Fred Morrow Fling—that history deals with the past as a whole, but not with the whole of the past. That must be the guiding ideal in the study and writing of history, regardless of the period selected for investigation.

In the process by which science operates, individual facts are assembled and classified according to likeness within the classes, and difference among classes. Arrangement into categories is accomplished by the application of selected criteria, the choice of these standards being governed by the purpose for which they are to be used. In other words, classification is subjective, relative, and functional, and is valid only within the frame of reference specified by such limiting factors. In general, these principles of scientific method apply to all the sciences, whether physical, biological, or social; or synthetic combinations of them.

But, more specifically, the product of such operations falls into two categories: objective and subjective relativism. In the former, which is emphasized in the natural sciences, to be accepted as valid the results of scientific investigation must be verifiable. In the latter, which is emphasized in the social sciences, and in history when defined as a social science, according to the philosophy of John Dewey, Charles Beard, and Carl Becker, verifiability is limited or even denied. According to this latter view all social science must necessarily be constructed according to a personally selected frame of reference, whether or not admitted, a condition which renders intellectual enterprise in this area subjective and uncertain. The resemblances of this point of view to that of the Greek Sophists are striking.

In science, the uniqueness of the individual item of fact is ignored or is subordinated to the formula of classification. As applied to facts about inanimate objects, or to plants and the lower animals, this may not appear to possess significance as a violation of individuality. But the principle of scientific procedure is the same as when applied to people. When dealt with scientifically, the human person is stripped of all his uniqueness. Science is amoral, and its method violates the uniqueness of all facts. So far as their absolute properties are concerned, all facts are distorted and falsified by science. Otherwise science's chosen purpose could not be achieved. Only the status of human persons as beings of an order of magnitude distinct from all others invests their fate at the hands of science with a special significance.

That scientists have gone too far in their generalization, classification, and laws is evident at mid-twentieth century. That area of science which is considered the most exact of all, mathematical physics, provides the best illustration, and is beautifully described by M. Born, with particular attention to Nels Bohr's principle of Complementarity. Born insists at the close of his article "Physics and Metaphysics" (*Scientific Monthly,* May 1956) that this principle possesses applicability outside of physics, in fact, "not only in philosophy but in all ways of life" when two kinds of expressions are necessary—when a single "description of the whole of a system in one picture is impossible; there are complementary images which do not apply simultaneously but are nevertheless not contradictory and exhaust the whole only together."

Pleistocene geology is of particular interest in connection with the thought pursued here, because the record is continuous into the present. Furthermore, during the latter part of Pleistocene time primitive man participated in making the geological record, because of his influence upon landscape. Indeed, the present is within the Pleistocene geological unit of time and so is the immediate future, so far as foreseeable. Also, the archeological record makes certain the long occupance of the earth by man during the later Pleistocene and the interrelations between man and landscape. Intensive study of this geological time-span is comparatively recent, but research has come to important conclusions.

The intimacy with which the Pleistocene formations may be studied forces the rejection of a large part of the generalization about geological process. Each spot emerges as unique, possessed of its own individual history. Much of this can be reconstructed and dated in remarkable detail. Most important to this theme of history is that in the Pleistocene the order of magnitude of geological and present time merge into one and the same thing, without discontinuity. The processes studied in geology or geological processes are still operating and in an order of magnitude significant to contemporary man's planning about the future of his occupance of the earth.

An example is found in the earth sciences in the case of W. M. Davis' cycle of erosion which holds that landscapes experience successive stages of youth, maturity, old age, and rejuvenation. But, in the field, particular landscapes have not been found to follow such a uniform pattern. Each area of the earth's surface has been subject to so many different variables, operating in unpredictable combinations, as to create unique physical formations with unique histories. Carl Sauer insists in his book *Agricultural Origins and Dispersals,* 1952, that the unreality of Davis' system has actually delayed learning about physical geography.

In ecology, which may be described as the study of organisms living together, the two major American schools of theory, those of E. F. Clements and of H. C. Cowles—particularly the former—were highly formalized. A 1954 product of this type of thinking about the North American grassland was summarized for review purposes as follows:

> The basic media of interpretation that appear throughout the work are the theories of the closed community, nattural succession, and climax. It is conceived that prior to the invasion of the white man the prairie consisted of essentially stable climax communities, ". . . the outcome of thousands of years of sorting of species and adaptations to soil and climate. Grassland soils through untold centuries have been thoroughly protected by the unbroken mantle of prairie vegetation." The author looks upon the prairie as ". . . much more than land covered with grass. It is a slowly evolved, highly complex organic entity, centuries old. It approaches the eternal. Once destroyed, it can never be replaced by man."

The reviewer who wrote the above, and an increasing number of other ecologists, repudiated these concepts of a finished world that had been destroyed by modern man. Vegetation was not an organism; the concept of natural succession leading to climax was not historically realistic. Disturbances from natural causes, and by primitive man, had repeatedly interrupted plant successions, even at times destroying the vegetational cover altogether—not once, but, in some places, repeatedly. H. A. Gleason had pioneered the individualistic concept of the plant association and a number of other realistic points of view about vegetation, but was largely ignored by his generation. Belatedly, ecologists have learned in the hard way the extent to which he was correct. Vegetation is an open system of change, subject to influences of many independent variables. Whether forest or grass cover, the vegetation of any particular spot possesses a unique history. Having been partially or wholly destroyed repeatedly, it has demonstrated a remarkable capacity to recuperate, always in a variant form.[1]

The soils of the North American grassland present another case to illustrate the issues under consideration. The reconstruction of the record of their history, with the aid of the tools of Pleistocene geological records, archeology, and ecology, demonstrates that soils of some areas have been destroyed and renewed repeatedly. To those records are added the verdict of the written record, to the same effect. Yet these soils were so productive when European man first occupied them that in his ignorance he called them "virgin" soils. They were the soils pictured as the product of "untold centuries." To be accurate about soils, each spot must be studied and its history reconstructed. Soils are not an organism

---

[1] The quotation is from Hugh M. Raup's review of John E. Weaver, "The North American Prairie" (1954), in *The Quarterly Review of Biology*, 30, June 1955, pp. 156–57. See also Frank E. Egler's review of the same book, *Ecology*, 37, January 1956, pp. 208–9. For literature on forests written from the similar point of view as these reviews, see the monographs by Hugh M. Raup and associates in the publications of the Harvard Forest Bulletins, Petersham, Massachusetts. H. A. Gleason's first paper formulating explicitly "The Individualistic Concept of the Plant Association," appeared in the *Bulletin* of the Torrey Botanical Club, 53, 1926, pp. 7–26.

experiencing life cycles of youth, maturity, and old age, but are an open system. The time factor in soil formation varies with the nature of the parent materials and circumstances, but upon occasion it has been demonstrated to be less than the life span of the men who may occupy the area. For some loessial materials the time factor for freshly exposed materials is zero.[2]

The anthropologist deals primarily with man prior to acquisition of the art of writing. Necessarily he deals with the anonymous, with human beings in groups according to some scheme of classification. The nature of the data compels such a technique. But, when he studies human cultures historically, except for these limitations imposed by the absence of individual identification, the anthropologist must operate as does the historian according to the conventional definition.

Each cultural group is unique and possesses distinguishing properties that are unique in the absolute sense, because they belong to a particular time, place,

---

[2] Waldo Wedel, "Environment and Native Subsistence Economies in the Central Great Plains," *Smithsonian Misc. Collections,* 101, No. 3; "Prehistory and Environment in the Central Great Plains," *Transactions of the Kansas Academy of Science,* 50, 1947, pp. 1–18; "Some Aspects of Human Ecology in the Central Plains," *American Anthropologist,* 55, 1953, pp. 499–514; Hans Jenny, *Factors in Soil Formation,* 1941, pp. 35–38; James C. Malin, "Dust Storms, 1850–1900," *Kansas Historical Quarterly,* 14, May, August, November 1946, pp. 129–44, 265–96, 391–413; *The Grassland of North America,* 1947, Chs. 8–10, and pp. 212–21; "Man, State of Nature and Climax . . . ," *Scientific Monthly,* 74, January 1952, pp. 29–37.

and people. These properties cannot be duplicated elsewhere, nor in the same place and population at another
time. The anthropologist, when writing the history of
cultures, is not a social scientist in search of laws, but a
historian reconstructing unique historical reality. So far
as he uses social science techniques of classification as
the basis of operation on a mass of anonymous data, he
is doing so as a historian. He is describing, in successive
periods of time and space, the changes in the states of
culture that took place under the multifactoral relations
in which the culture or cultures in question operated.
Within the limitations stated, this operation might be
called historical social science or historical sociology.
But the terms social science and sociology have been
used in so many ways, mostly in a context of social
laws, recurring cycles, social planning, etc., that few
would probably differentiate from these the limited
meaning here set forth. These reasons seem adequate
to justify the use of a different term—"cultural history," as more meaningful for the historical operation
of the anthropologist.

In anthropogeography, where the natural and the
human record are merged, Carl Sauer has again spoken
out plainly. In his *Agricultural Origins and Dispersals*
he rejects the use of the terms science and social science
and uses natural history and cultural history: "The
things with which we are concerned are changing continuously and without end, and they take place, for
good reason, not anywhere, but somewhere; that is, in

actual situations or places. That succession of events . . . is quite other than the conceptual models that are set up as regular, recurrent, or parallel stages and cycles."[3]

In the field of geography in its more traditional sense, and in contradistinction to the systematic approach based upon classification and generalization, Derwent Whittlesey maintains that the essence of geography lies in differentiation of areas of the earth's surface. Of course, the heart of this argument is the insistence upon uniqueness of each and every area that might be selected as an object of study. Only in description of "the entire content of the human occupance of the area," and in differentiation of it from other areas, is knowledge about geography effective.[4] Differentiation describes without indulging in value judgments, functionalism, or planning.

In biology, the discovery of chromosomes and genes opened the way to new concepts of genetics. Carried into the field of taxonomy, biologists emphasize the genetic uniqueness of every unit in a population classed for systematic purposes into genera and species. These

---

[3] Carl Sauer, *Agricultural Origins and Dispersals*, p. 2.

[4] Derwent Whittlesey, "The Regional Concept and the Regional Method," P. E. James and C. F. Jones (Editors), *American Geography: Inventory and Prospect* (New York: Syracuse University Press, 1954), 19–68; "Southern Rhodesia—An African Compage," *Annals of the Association of American Geographers*, 46, March 1956, pp. 1–97.

individual differences are absolute and a knowledge of them has worked a revolution in the concepts of genetics. The ramifications of so remarkable a principle are yet scarcely explored.

Thus it is clear that among the sciences, primary and synthetic, a significant challenge has been registered against overemphasis upon generalization, upon laws, upon cyclic repetition, and prediction. There has been more than a protest. Among the more independent and creative minds new paths have been marked out and important innovations introduced and demonstrated in both theory and practice. Uniqueness of facts and combinations of them defy classification, and for certain areas of knowledge the theory and structure of science must be reconstructed in accordance with the principle of uniqueness. Particularly this has occurred in the field, as distinguished from the laboratory, sciences. But while these developments have been conspicuous in the sciences, so-called, substantially the opposite has occurred in the social sciences, and even history is claimed as a social science.

The attempted transformation of history into a social science came about under the influence of John Dewey and others of the so-called pragmatic group of philosophy and ethics; and under the influence of Charles Beard, James Harvey Robinson, and Carl Becker in history. The philosophy of Benedetto Croce was drawn upon also. Subjective relativism, with its emphasis upon

presentism, functionalism, and social planning, became
the watchwords of history as social science—to make
good citizens and good Americans. The path they pioneered was then written into the fabric of educational
thought and practice by a series of committees. The
nihilism of their skepticism was as complete as that of
the Greek Sophists, but without benefit of a Socrates to
insist upon the validity of ethical principles.[5]

The committee that prepared Social Science Research Council *Bulletin* 64 expressly repudiated (pp.
26-27n.) the uniqueness of history, holding that the
insistence by "certain German historiographers" upon
the unique in history "appears to rest in part upon

[5] National Education Association, Educational Policies Commission,
The Unique Function of Education in American Democracy (Washington, 1937); American Historical Association Commission on
social studies in the schools (appointed, 1928), report in 16 volumes,
two of which are of particular importance to the present discussion:
A Charter for the Social Sciences, 1932, and *Conclusions and Rec-
ommendations,* 1934. Charles Beard had a conspicuous hand in both
of these commissions and their product. The Social Science Research
Council, *Bulletin 54, Theory and Practice in Historical Study: A
Report of the Committee on Historiography,* 1946, Merle Curti,
chairman; *Bulletin 64, The Social Sciences in Historical Study: A
Report of the Committee on Historiography,* 1954. Charles Beard
was a member of the committee that prepared *Bulletin 54,* the other
members being his or Carl Becker's disciples. The members of the
committee that prepared *Bulletin 64* were similarly committed in
their ideology.

The differing views of the present writer are to be found particularly in *Essays on Historiography,* 1946, *On the Nature of History,*
1954, and *The Contriving Brain and the Skillful Hand in the United
States,* 1955, all privately printed by the author.

faulty logic and in part upon a semantic confusion over the term unique." Likewise in the section on anthropology (pp. 35-41) the committee ignored Carl Sauer's insistence that in cultural history things happen in "nonduplicated time and place," and change "continuously and without end, and take place, for good reason, not anywhere, but somewhere, that is in actual situations or places."

The historian's task is differentiation rather than the formulation of sociological generalizations. Difference is an absolute, while the similarities emphasized by sociological classifications are subjectively relative. Once the full significance of that fact is clearly grasped, the whole orientation of the student of history is changed in a manner that is fundamental. Even though the historian has not proved as successful as he might be in isolating the properties of uniqueness of the individual, or of history, or of other absolutes within his province, yet to be clearly conscious of the nature of his task as intellectual enterprise is an important achievement—in fact, a major one. Having accomplished that, he can never again think of history as a social science.

The degree to which social historians came to look upon themselves as twentieth-century counterparts of the French *Philosophes* of the eighteenth century is emphasized by Carl Becker's *The Heavenly City of the Eighteenth Century Philosophers* (1932), and the reception it received during the nineteen-thirties and after.[6] Certain of the *Philosophes,* the most conspicuous of whom was Voltaire, turned to what they called history, really sociology or social science and a-historical, with the purpose of revealing the laws of nature. The twentieth-century historians who looked upon history as social science were similarly obsessed with the determination to make history useful in transforming the world to conform to their heart's desire— some form of collectivism.

Of course, the eighteenth century, which mid-twentieth-century historians after Becker began to call the Enlightenment, was really quite different in England, in the United States, in France, and in Germany. Even in his enthusiasm for eighteenth-century France, Becker admitted that few *Philosophes* were original thinkers, and that their significance lay in their role as popularizers. The sixteenth and the seventeenth centuries had been creative, and to some extent this continued in England during the eighteenth century. In the Germanies a great scientific, literary, and philosophical flowering occurred near the end of the eighteenth and in the early nineteenth centuries. But the enthusiasm of Americans of the mid-twentieth century for the miscalled Enlightenment of the eighteenth century centered upon the United States and France, and particularly upon sociological generalizations. Implicit in

---

[6] Malin, *The Contriving Brain and the Skillful Hand*, pp. 348–92.

their inexorable law of nature was the idea of a finished world—nature is good and only man is vile. So far as the doctrine of the perfectibility of man was concerned, he was to be brought by reason into harmony with nature and nature's God. Man, nature, equality, etc., were abstractions—sociological generalizations in a never-never land.

The extent of this grounding of historical and social science thought of the United States in eighteenth-century confusion may be illustrated by two books: Arthur A. Ekirch, *The Decline of American Liberalism* (1955), and Eric Goldman, *Rendezvous with Destiny* (1952). In explaining his understanding of liberalism, Ekirch asserts that "the eighteenth century was its classic age" (p. 11), and made these eighteenth-century formulations his measuring stick for all that came after.

The formula adopted by Goldman was to label the liberal reformers "by the terms they applied to themselves [p. viii]." For the most part these self-styled liberals were actually pursuing their private interpretations of the eighteenth-century phantoms. Thus Ekirch and Goldman did not really disagree materially about what they considered fundamentals although they got at them by different routes. Both are subjective relativists, finding the same basic frame of reference in the "Golden Age" of the eighteenth-century sociological formulas. But social science classifications and generalizations possess only a limited validity which is determined by the criteria, and the use in a particular time and place, for which they are devised. In other words, they are not valid any time, any where, and the attempt so to apply them predetermines the outcome. In these particular cases liberalism necessarily declined. History is concerned with change; so, inevitably, times were soon out of joint in terms of these eighteenth-century absolutes. To save themselves, some self-styled liberals, without abandoning candidly their antiquated absolutes, undertook to redefine liberalism in such a manner as virtually to reverse the eighteenth-century formula. That both liberals and conservatives of the twentieth century are confused is not a matter of wonder, especially when account is taken also of the further contradictions introduced into the undigested eclectic conglomerate during the nineteenth century from the work of Malthus, Ricardo, Spencer, Darwin, Huxley, Mendel, etc., all of which discarded biological equality.

The concept of equalitarianism has a long history, but in any case it is a social science term which by the process of classification emphasizes likenesses at the expense of difference. In the eighteenth century it was imputed the quality of an absolute and was incorporated into the Declaration of Independence of the United States in that unqualified form—"All men are created equal." As no attempt was made to define the meaning in terms of criteria and use, each individual, according to his own frame of reference, was left to his own private rationalization. In the hands of extremists equality is misused as an absolute in violation of the dignity of the unique properties of the individual. At best, the concept of equality is an approximation, statistical in character, and of limited applicability. It is not a right or a property of individuality, nor the basis for any claim of primary right. Any utility or validity it ever possessed was as a derived mental construct applicable to a particular time and place. At worst, the concept of equality is an outrage upon human dignity.

The impact of the contradictions between the Finished World of the eighteenth century and the Evolutionary World of the late nineteenth century calls for some explanation. In the alleged eighteenth-century climax of liberalism, the Age of Reason, and the state of nature, only man was vile. But this static eighteenth-century mythical world was irreconcilable with the evolutionary world of Spencer, Huxley, and Darwin, of science and philosophy a century after—not equality, but survival of the "fittest." According to their eclectic habits, Americans operating in the areas of natural history and natural science failed to realize all the implications of the conflict. The difference between the two modes of thought was absolute. Among other difficulties, religious traditions injected an emotional block to logical intellectual processes.

The particular background of the finished-world notion was to be found in the Christian concept of the Garden of Eden, the fall of man, and his redemption by divine intervention—the blood sacrifice. Eighteenth-century rationalism substituted the state of nature for the Garden of Eden, man's violation of nature for the fall of man, and the doctrine of progress, the unlimited perfectibility of man through his own efforts, for redemption by divine intervention. Basically the only difference between the eighteenth-century "Enlightenment" and Christianity was the mode of redemption— but that difference was unbridgeable. The evolutionism of the late nineteenth century challenged both systems —no Garden of Eden, no fall of man, therefore no redemption was necessary. Most evolutionists were not successful, however, in achieving a complete breakthrough into a truly open system. With few exceptions, evolutionists were still committed to fatal remnants of the old systems, including a teleology which made man the end-product. In a truly open system there is no end-product, for then the system would not be open. Man's concern is with the dignity of man as a unique sentient being and his potentiality to achieve a new order of magnitude of actuality—but to specify is to limit by the very indication of an implied teleological goal. In an "open system" the potentiality is unpredictable; the prime absolute is that potentiality becomes unique indeterminate actuality.

Early twentieth-century American ecologists, the "classical" schools of Clements and Cowles, were victims of this conflict between eighteenth- and nineteenth-century thought. Although under the illusion that they accepted evolution, they retained their eighteenth-century nature concepts: natural succession, they insisted, led to climax formation—an inexorable law of nature if "civilized" (no longer in the state of nature) man did not intervene and destroy nature's finished handiwork. That they were not conscious of the paradox and were unaware of the source of their ideas is immaterial to the present discussion. The American conservation movement, as it took shape during the late nineteenth and the early twentieth centuries, was conspicuously emotional rather than intellectual and was wholly committed to a similar, basic paradox formula, although arrived at by a route somewhat different from that of the ecologists. The formula, an eclectic conglomerate of contradictions, was a propaganda natural for several types of short-term demagoguery, which diverted attention from essentials.

Differentiation and uniqueness are among the fundamentals at the basis of the theory and practice of history. Differentiation does not necessarily involve value judgments. Differences among spaces on the earth, among objects in nature, among persons, and among these at separate points in time, reveal the fact that each in space and time is unique and in an absolute sense. To the argument that the designation of uniqueness is itself classification, a sufficient answer should be that the two are not of the same order of magnitude. Uniqueness is an absolute both in theory and in verification, while classification is relative to the selected criteria applied to all units in a class.

The quest for a formulation of a theory of history in

its absolute character of uniqueness must determine the properties of the individual. Every object in nature possesses properties, but the human individual possesses additional properties that distinguish him as a unique entity—intellectual curiosity, and potentiality being among his singularities. By properties is meant the essential characteristics without which he could not exist and be identified. These properties, to qualify as such, must not be derived from any subjective frame of reference, but must be independent of any particular culture, and of space and time. So far as any particular formulation of the properties of the individual person fails in that respect, the fault lies with the formulation and not with the concept of properties, nor with the concept of uniqueness. These properties must identify and describe the dignity of the human person, which is absolute. The person's right of defense of his status in society and of his ethical principles must be based upon his uniqueness inherent in these properties. Human history is the unique record of the singularity of every individual person.

The singularity of the individual is demonstrated biologically according to the genetic principles of chromosomes, genes, etc. This individual difference is absolute.[7]

---

[7] Edgar Anderson, geneticist, has stressed in the taxonomy of plants that the whole concept of genes and species must recognize the uniqueness of each individual. Roger J. Williams, chemist, in *Free*

The human individual, in addition, possesses a contriving brain; insatiable intellectual curiosity, regardless of utility; a memory; the power to reason; the capacity to order facts for long-range utilization; purpose; the will to make decisions and a capacity to execute them in subtle ways. All of these qualities are possessed by man at an order of magnitude which differentiates him absolutely from other animals. How this status was achieved, he does not know, but the individual person knows that it did happen. And more, man possessed potentiality, a power to realize his potentiality in actuality; a power to which no limit is known. This property of the individual person has been the theme of the world's best minds through all ages. Aristotle opened his *Metaphysica* with the dictum: "All men by nature desire to know," and in *De Anima* he asserted that mind "can have no nature of its own, other than that of a certain capacity." Also, "everything is a possible object of thought." About a millennium and a half later St. Thomas Aquinas gave the idea its most effective reformulation: "Therefore infinity is potentially in our minds through its consider-

---

and Unequal (Austin: University of Texas Press, 1953), has emphasized the biochemical uniqueness of every person and the importance to medicine of a recognition of the fact. As among human subspecies, E. Raymond Hall has insisted upon their unique properties even in international political relations: "Zoological Subspecies of Man at the Peace Table," *Journal of Mammology,* 27, November 1946, pp. 358–64.

ing successively one thing after another, because never does the intellect understand so many things, that it cannot understand more."[8]

As an academic discipline, anthropology practices a dual role that has not been accurately recognized and differentiated—that of cultural history and that of social science. As cultural history it is concerned as vitally with uniqueness as is any other aspect of history. Although dealing with unidentified individuals, certain data may be so ordered as to describe groups of individuals and conditions as they change continuously at particular points in space and time. Such descriptions are history, cultural history in the sense in which Carl Sauer used the term; or for those who insist upon using other terminology, they are historical social science or historical sociology, in the same sense that the geologist uses the term historical geology or historical geomorphology, or historical paleontology, paleobotany, or paleoecology.

There is no sound reason why the methods of the anthropogeographer employed in those areas for anonymous data may not also be applied to more recent

---

[8] The edition of *The Works of Aristotle* used here is that translated into English and edited by J. A. Smith, and W. D. Ross (Oxford: Oxford University Press), the *Physica,* by R. P. Hardie, and R. K. Gage, 1930; the *Metaphysica,* by W. D. Ross, 1908; *De Anima,* by J. A. Smith, 1931. The translation of the *Summa Theologica* used here is that of the Fathers of the English Dominican Province, 1912. For a fuller discussion, Malin, *The Contriving Brain and the Skillful Hand,* Ch. 11.

data. But, in any case, the end-product is the description of uniqueness of the group, or groups, their structure or behavior at specified points of space and time, and when arranged in time sequences such description may be effective reconstructions of historical sequences —social history or, more accurately, cultural history, using the word culture in the anthropologist's sense. As the object of history as applied to human beings must necessarily be the differentiation of uniqueness among persons, this cultural history based upon group data must give precedence to history based upon the identifiable individual person as soon as the written documents become available for that purpose. And from that point forward in time, the group data become secondary or supplemental to history in terms of the unique individual.

In history, written faithfully according to the principle of the unique, the question of conservatism and liberalism is not at issue. Those currently indoctrinated in the sociological concepts of liberalism and conservatism, and the subjective-relativist frame-of-reference philosophy, are prone to reject the principle of the uniqueness of the individual and of history. In their commitment to the either/or form of logic they cannot admit that it is possible to act upon any other basis, or with objective integrity, or even an approximation thereof. No one could be more dangerous, to either of the respective sociological generalizations of extremes, than the stubborn historian, with his insistence upon the unique properties of history and of the person. To be unique, to recognize it and to act consistently upon it, is to be alone and lonely in a world committed to groupthink, regardless of the name by which it is called. The fact of uniqueness and the generalizations about liberalism and conservatism are of wholly different orders of magnitude and are irreconcilable.

The basic thinking of modern times has been performed, not by the United States or Russia, but by western and central Europe. That historic fact should focus attention upon the critical question of the conditions under which the creativity of the contriving brains of men operate. How much does cultural environment contribute and how much is originality the unpredictable product of the unique person, even in spite of surrounding conditions? The features of the history of the United States which American historians boast about—the open frontier, democracy, equalitarianism, and mass education—have thus far produced little that could qualify as basic thinking. Technology is quite another matter. The uniqueness of history precludes laws, predictability, and planning, because those technological concepts and originality are a contradiction of terms.

How is freedom of the individual in society to be defined? Under what condition may he realize his fullest potentiality? The most widely publicized formulation of the twentieth century was the so-called Four Freedoms, promulgated in 1941: freedom of speech and of religion, and freedom from want and fear. A cynical cartoonist pictured animals in a zoo that could enjoy all four freedoms yet be locked in a cage. Of a fundamental character, however, were the four freedoms of the priests of Apollo at Delphi some 200 years B.C. The differences between freedom and slavery then were described as consisting of a protected legal status in society, personal inviolability (freedom from seizure or arrest), freedom of economic activity, and the right of unrestricted movement in space. Some two thousand years of experience have not subtracted anything from that formula.[9]

The most that can be done, probably, toward promoting creativity is to provide unique minds with freedom to realize their potentialities. The question is in order whether or not, for this purpose, form of government *per se* is even relevant. It is difficult to see how captivity to the errors of eighteenth-century sociological generalizations can contribute to originality. Planned and subsidized "research" monopolizes time and energy of competent minds that might otherwise accomplish something creative. It is thought control. A concept of scholarship that has been conspicuous in Europe is that the body of human knowledge possesses value in its own right, and is to be pursued for itself as an object

---

[9] William L. Westermann, "Between Slavery and Freedom," *American Historical Review,* 50, January 1945, pp. 213–27.

of study, and without respect to any functionalism or usefulness to which it may be put. By contrast, the attitude toward human knowledge conspicuous among American subjective relativists, and foremost is SSRC *Bulletins* 54 and 64, is that only such fragments of it are worth knowing as are "useful" to some present purpose in the mind of the social science historian, or other social scientist.

One approach is comprehensive and uncommitted, the other is restricted, selective, programmatic, its functionalism being determined by some supposed "usefulness" in the ephemeral present of the investigator. The results of the practice of uncommitted scholarship in any field, however, are often productive of something that is actually and unexpectedly more useful than studies undertaken with a functional purpose. The reason is not difficult to seek, because the exploration of a subject in all its relatedness may succeed in turning up the unpredictable meanings. Also, this attitude toward knowledge, in not being committed beforehand to a purpose, may be truly discriminative. Instead of directing hostility toward and ridicule at the so-called ivory tower, that position of objective isolation should be recognized by social scientists as critical to all sound social policy studies.

In history, as in other intellectual enterprise, uncommitted investigation is primary, not derivative, and its objectivity alone affords the conditions conducive to a high order of reflective thought. Basic thinking is primary, technological application or functionalism is derivative. Freedom of the mind and functional commitments are contradictory and mutually exclusive, because commitment imposes limitations. Only in an uncommitted orientation can the mind be truly free.

Capitalism
and Freedom

Milton Friedman

Milton Friedman, 1976 Nobel laureate in economics, is Paul Snowden Russell Distinguished Service Professor of Economics at the University of Chicago. A past president of the American Economic Association, Professor Friedman was awarded the John Bates Clark medal of that association in 1951. Among his best-known books are Capitalism and Freedom *and (with Anna J. Schwartz)* A Monetary History of the United States, 1867–1960.

This paper deals with the relation between the freedom enjoyed by individuals in a society and the form of economic organization adopted by that society. Its thesis is that a necessary condition for individual freedom is the organization of the bulk of economic activity through private enterprises operating in a free market—a form of organization I shall refer to as competitive capitalism. While necessary for freedom, capitalism alone is not sufficient to guarantee freedom. It must be accompanied by a set of values and by political institutions favorable to freedom; these additional requirements are not considered in this paper.

The economic system plays a dual role in promoting freedom. In the first place, economic freedom is itself an essential component of freedom in general. Competitive capitalism, as the system most favorable to economic freedom, is for this reason an end in itself. In the second place, economic freedom is a means toward political or civil freedom. By permitting an effective separation of economic from political power, it reduces the costs of political idiosyncrasy, and provides numerous independent foci of potential opposition to the suppression of freedom. Historical experience and logical analysis alike support this thesis.

The growth and spread of civil freedom in the West clearly coincided with the spread of capitalism as the dominant system of economic organization. I know of no example of a society, at any time or place, definable as a free society, that did not use a predominantly private market system to organize its economic activities. Equally clearly, capitalism alone has not been enough to guarantee freedom. Japan, at least prior to World War II, and Russia, prior to World War I, were capitalist societies, yet essentially autocratic in political structure. Fascist Italy and contemporary Spain are additional examples, though somewhat less clear ones; in both, the state has played such a large role in controlling and conducting economic affairs that it is perhaps better to describe them as socialist or collectivist societies than as capitalist. And this is surely so for National Socialist Germany.

Yet it is noteworthy that even in these countries—Nazi Germany alone excepted—suppression of individual freedom has gone nothing like so far as in the modern totalitarian regimes of Russia and China, where economic collectivism is combined with political authoritarianism and where little more than vestiges of capitalism survive. The reason seems clear. Such capitalism as there was provided some sources of power partly independent of the overriding political authorities. In addition, of course, capitalism meant some measure of economic freedom—so that the subjects of even Czarist Russia could change some jobs without permission of an instrumentality of the state.

The relation between economic freedom and political freedom is complex and by no means unilateral. In early nineteenth-century England, the philosophical radicals and their allies regarded political reform as primarily a means toward economic freedom. Following Adam Smith, Ricardo, and Bentham, they believed that a reduction of state intervention in economic affairs, a large measure of *laissez faire,* was the main requisite for rapid economic progress and the wide distribution of its fruits among the masses—and, as an aside, subsequent experience under a largely *laissez faire* regime gives no reason to doubt the correctness of their belief. These early liberals viewed the vested interests of the politically powerful, particularly the landowners, as the chief obstacle to such a policy. Political reform would give the power to the people and the people would naturally legislate in their own interest, which is to say, would legislate *laissez faire.*

From the end of the nineteenth century to the present, the leading liberal writers—men like Dicey, Mises, Hayek, and Simons, to mention only a few—emphasized the reverse relation: that economic freedom is a means toward political freedom. The triumph of Benthamite liberalism in nineteenth-century England was followed by government in economic affairs, and this tendency to collectivism was greatly accelerated both in Great Britain and elsewhere by the two world wars. Welfare, rather than freedom, became the dominant note in democratic countries. Recognizing the implicit threat to individualism, these writers feared that a continued movement toward centralized control of economic activity would prove *The Road to Serfdom,* as Hayek entitled his penetrating analysis of the process.

Events since the end of World War II display a still different relation between economic and political freedom. Collectivist economic planning has indeed interfered with individual freedom. At least in some countries, however, the result has not been the suppression of freedom, but the reversal of economic policy. England again provides the most striking example. The turning point is perhaps the "control of engagements" order which, despite great misgivings, the Labor Party found it necessary to impose in order to carry out its economic policy. Fully enforced and carried through, the law would have involved centralized allocation of individuals to occupations. But this conflicted so sharply with personal liberty that it was enforced in a negligible number of cases and repealed after the law had been in effect for only a short period. Its repeal ushered in a decided shift in economic policy, marked by reduced reliance on centralized "plans" and "programs," by the dismantling of many controls, and by increased emphasis on the private market. A similar shift in policy occurred in most other democratic countries. The proximate explanation of these shifts in policy is the limited success or outright failure of central planning to achieve its stated objectives. However, this failure is itself to be attributed, at least in some measure, to the political implications of central planning and to an unwillingness to follow out its logic when so doing requires roughshod trampling on treasured private rights. It may well be that the shift is only a temporary interruption to the collectivist trend of this century. Even so, it illustrates strikingly the close relation between political freedom and economic arrangements.

Adam Smith saw clearly that the effective utilization of economic resources requires the coordination of large numbers of people. As he phrased it, "division of labor is limited by the extent of the market." The developments in population and technology since he wrote have continuously expanded the scale on which coordination is required to take full advantage of modern science. It is trite to note that literally millions of people are involved in providing one another with their daily bread, let alone with their yearly automobiles. The challenge to the believer in liberty is to reconcile this widespread interdependence with individual freedom.

Fundamentally, there are only two ways of coordinating the economic activities of millions. One is central direction involving use of coercion—the technique of the modern totalitarian state. The other is voluntary cooperation of individuals—the technique of the market place.

The possibility of coordination through voluntary cooperation rests on the elementary—yet frequently denied—proposition that both parties to an economic transaction benefit from it *provided that the transaction is bilaterally voluntary and informed.* Exchange can therefore bring about coordination without coercion. A working model of a society organized through voluntary exchange is a *free private enterprise exchange economy*—what we have been calling competitive capitalism.

In its simplest form, such a society consists of a number of independent households—a collection of Robinson Crusoes, as it were. Each household uses the resources it controls to produce goods and services that it exchanges for goods and services produced by other households on terms mutually acceptable to the two parties to the bargain. It is thereby enabled to satisfy its wants indirectly by producing goods and services that other households ultimately use rather than directly by producing goods for its own immediate use. The incentive for adopting this indirect route is, of course, the increased "output" made possible by division of labor and specialization of function. In consequence, both parties can benefit from each exchange.

Since the household always has the alternative of producing directly for itself, it need not enter into any exchange unless it does benefit, so no exchange will take place unless both parties benefit from it. Cooperation is thereby achieved without coercion.

Division of labor and specialization of function could not go far in a simple exchange economy in which a household is the largest productive unit and in which final products are exchanged against final products. To extend the scope of division of labor, the productive unit in existing market economies is largely separated from the consumption unit. It takes the form of an enterprise that serves as an intermediary between the use of the resources owned by some households to produce products, and the acquisition of the products by the same or other households. The introduction of such an intermediary permits cooperation in production over a far broader area and makes possible complex chains of exchanges and indirect means of utilizing resources. The elaboration of cooperative arrangements is further facilitated by the use of "money," or generalized purchasing power, to effect transactions rather than the direct exchange of goods or services.

Despite the important role of enterprises and of money in our actual economy, and despite the numerous and complex problems they raise, the central characteristics of the market technique of achieving coordination is fully displayed in the simple exchange economy that contains neither enterprises nor money.

As in that simple model, so in the complex enterprise and money-exchange economy, cooperation is strictly individual and voluntary *provided* (a) that enterprises are private, so that the ultimate contracting parties are individuals and (b) that individuals are effectively free to enter or not to enter into any particular exchange, so that every transaction is strictly voluntary.

It is far easier to state these provisos in general terms than to spell them out in detail, or to specify precisely the institutional arrangements most conducive to their maintenance. Indeed, much of technical economic literature is concerned with precisely these questions. The basic requisite is the maintenance of law and order to prevent physical coercion of one individual by another and to enforce contracts voluntarily entered into, thus giving content to "private." Aside from this, perhaps the most difficult problems arise from "monopoly"— which inhibits effective freedom by denying individuals alternatives to the particular exchange—and from "neighborhood effects"—effects on third parties for which it is not feasible to charge or recompense them.

Though full discussion is not possible here, the range of problems involved is suggested by the divergent meaning attributed to "free" as an adjective modifying enterprise. One meaning, the one that has generally been given to it in continental Europe, is that "enterprises" shall be free to do what they want, including fixing prices, dividing markets, and adopting other techniques to keep out potential competitors. Another, inherent in British thought and American law and tradition, is that anyone shall be "free" to set up an enterprise, which means that existing enterprises are not "free" to keep competitors out except by selling a better product at the same price, or the same product at a lower price. The European conception is a natural outgrowth of a "status" society; the American, of a democratic and equalitarian society. And the different conceptions have in their turn reacted on the character of the society; the European conception fostering a structured economy, economic "classes," and an industrial aristocracy to complement its social aristocracy; the American conception fostering economic mobility, classlessness, and economic democracy to complement its social democracy.

So long as effective freedom of exchange is maintained, the central feature of the market organization of economic activity is that it prevents one person from interfering with another in respect of most of his activities. The consumer is protected from coercion by the seller because of the presence of other sellers with whom he can deal. The seller is protected from coercion by the consumer because of other consumers to whom he can sell. The employee is protected from coercion by the employer because of other employers for whom he can work, and so on. And the market does this impersonally and without any centralized authority.

Indeed, a major source of objections to a free economy is precisely that it does this task so well. It gives people what they want instead of what a particular group thinks they ought to want. Underlying most arguments against the free market is a lack of belief in freedom itself.

The economic freedoms provided by the market include the freedom to starve, to use the phrase with which enemies of the market delight to attack it. The market guarantees an individual the freedom to make the most of the resources he happens to own, provided only that he does not interfere with the freedom of anyone else to do the same. But it does not guarantee that he will own the same amount of resources as anyone else. The resources he happens to own reflect largely the accidents of birth, inheritance, and prior good or bad fortune. And there is nothing to prevent these from leading to wide disparities in wealth and income. These disparities are morally repugnant to many people and raise difficult ethical issues that cannot be explored here. They also serve very real functions, one of which will be noted later in this paper.

Insofar as disparities arise from monopoly, and similar market imperfections, they would be reduced by a closer approach to an ideal free market. But it must be recognized that even an ideal free market is consistent with wide inequality. Individual charity aside, there is no way of eliminating such differences in wealth as would remain in an ideal free market, except by interfering with the freedom of the more fortunate. It is a trite, if unpalatable, observation that freedom and egalitarianism can be inconsistent objectives. Fortunately, in practice they have proved not to be. Historically, a free market has produced less inequality, a wider distribution of wealth, and less poverty than any other form of economic organization. There is less inequality in advanced capitalist countries, like the United States, than in underdeveloped countries, like India.

Though paucity of data makes it difficult to be sure, there appears also to be less inequality in capitalist countries in general than in collectivist countries like Russia and China. In principle, collectivist societies could achieve substantial equality—albeit at the sacrifice of total output; in practice, they have not done so or even tried to do so.

The existence of a free market does not of course eliminate the need for government. On the contrary, as already noted, government is essential both as a forum for determining the "rules of the game" and as an umpire to interpret and enforce the rules decided on. What the market does is to reduce greatly the range of issues that must be decided through political means and thereby to minimize the extent to which government need participate directly in the game. The characteristic feature of action through political channels is that it tends to require or enforce substantial conformity. The great advantage of the market, on the other hand, is that it permits wide diversity. It is, in political terms, a system of proportional representation. Each man can vote, as it were, for the color of tie he wants and get it; he does not have to see what color the majority wants and then, if he is in the minority, submit.

It is this characteristic of the market that we refer to when we say that the market provides economic freedom. But this characteristic also has implications that go far beyond the narrowly economic. Political freedom means the absence of coercion of a man by his fellow men. The fundamental threat to freedom is power to coerce, be it in the hands of a monarch, a dictator, an oligarchy, or a momentary majority. The preservation of freedom requires the elimination of such concentrated power to the fullest possible extent and the dispersal and distribution of whatever power cannot be eliminated—a system of checks and balances. By removing the organization of economic activity from the control of political authority, the market eliminates this source of coercive power. It enables economic strength to be a check to political power rather than a reinforcement.

Economic strength is capable of being widely dispersed, for there is no law of conservation which forces the growth of new centers of economic strength to be at the expense of existing centers. There can simply be a larger number of millionaires, so to speak. Political power, on the other hand, is far more difficult to decentralize. Its personal character imposes something more nearly akin to a law of conservation of power. There can be numerous small independent governments. But it is far more difficult to maintain numerous equipotent small centers of political power in a single large government, as there can be numerous centers of economic strength in a single large economy. In consequence, if economic strength is joined to political power, concentration seems almost inevitable.

The force of this abstract argument can perhaps be demonstrated best by example. One feature of a free society is surely the freedom of individuals to advocate and propagandize openly for a radical change in the structure of the society—so long as the advocacy is restricted to persuasion and does not include force or other forms of coercion. It is a mark of the political freedom of a capitalist society that men can openly advocate and work for socialism. Equally, political freedom in a socialist society would require that men be free to advocate the introduction of capitalism. How could the freedom to advocate capitalism be preserved and protected in a socialist society?

In order for men to advocate anything they must in the first place be able to earn a living. This already raises a problem for a socialist society, since all jobs are under the direct control of political authorities. It would take an act of governmental self-denial whose difficulty is underlined by experience in the United States after World War II with the problem of "security" among federal employees, for a socialist government to permit its employees to advocate policies directly contrary to official doctrine.

But let us suppose this act of self-denial to be achieved. For advocacy of capitalism to mean anything, the proponents must be able to finance their cause—to hold public meetings, publish pamphlets, buy radio time, issue newspapers and magazines, and so on. How could they raise the funds? There might and probably would be men in the socialist society with large incomes, perhaps even large capital sums in the form of government bonds and the like, but these would of necessity be high public officials. It is possible to conceive of a minor socialist official retaining his job although openly advocating capitalism. It stretches credulity to imagine the socialist top brass financing such "subversive" activities.

The only recourse for funds would be to raise small amounts from a large number of minor officials. But this is no real answer. To tap these sources, many people would already have to be persuaded, and our whole problem is how to initiate and finance a campaign to do so. Radical movements in capitalist societies have never been financed this way. They have typically been supported by a few wealthy individuals who have become persuaded—by a Frederick Vanderbilt Field, or an Anita Blaine McCormick, or a Corliss Lamont, to mention a few names recently prominent, or by a Friedrich Engels, to go farther back. This is a role of inequality of wealth in preserving political freedom that is seldom noted—the role of the patron.

In a capitalist society, it is only necessary to persuade a few wealthy people to get funds to launch any idea, however strange, and there are many such persons, many independent foci of support. And, indeed, it is not even necessary to persuade people or financial institutions with available funds of the soundness of the ideas to be propagated. It is only necessary to persuade them that the propagation can be financially successful; that the newspaper or magazine or book or other venture will be profitable. The competitive publisher, for example, cannot afford to publish only writings with which he personally agrees; his touchstone must be the likelihood that the market will be large enough to yield a satisfactory return on his investment.

In this way, the market breaks the vicious circle and makes it possible ultimately to finance such ventures by small amounts from many people without first persuading them. There are no such possibilities in the socialist society; there is only the all-powerful state.

Let us stretch our imagination and suppose that a socialist government is aware of this problem and composed of people anxious to preserve freedom. Could it provide the funds? Perhaps, but it is difficult to see how. It could establish a bureau for subsidizing subversive propaganda. But how could it choose whom to support. If it gave to all who asked, it would shortly find itself out of funds, for socialism cannot repeal the elementary economic law that a sufficiently high price will call forth a large supply. Make the advocacy of radical causes sufficiently remunerative, and the supply of advocates will be unlimited.

Moreover, freedom to advocate unpopular causes does not require that such advocacy be without cost. On the contrary, no society could be stable, if advocacy of radical change were costless, much less subsidized. It is entirely appropriate that men make sacrifices to advocate causes in which they deeply believe. Indeed, it is important to preserve freedom only for people who are willing to practice self-denial, for otherwise freedom degenerates into license and irresponsibility. What is essential is that the cost of advocating unpopular causes be tolerable and not prohibitive.

But we are not yet through. In a free market society, it is enough to have the funds. The suppliers of paper are as willing to sell it to the *Daily Worker* as to the *Wall Street Journal*. In a socialist society, it would not be enough to have the funds. Our hypothetical capitalist organ would have to persuade the government factory making paper to sell to them, the government printing plant to print the paper, and so on.

Another example of the role of the market in preserving political freedom, and one that is closer to home, was revealed in our experience with McCarthyism. Entirely aside from the substantive issues involved, and the merits of the charges made, what

protection did individuals, and in particular government employees, have against irresponsible accusations
and probings into matters that it went against their
conscience to reveal? Their appeal to the Fifth Amendment would have been a hollow mockery without an
alternative to government employment.

Their fundamental protection was the existence of
a private market economy in which they could earn a
living. Here again, the protection was not absolute.
Many potential private employers were, rightly or
wrongly, adverse to hiring those pilloried. It may well
be that there was far less justification for the costs imposed on many of the people involved than for the
costs generally imposed on people who advocate unpopular causes. But the important point is that the costs
were limited and not prohibitive, as they would have
been if government employment had been the only
possibility.

It is of interest to note that a disproportionately
large fraction of the people involved apparently went
into the most competitive sectors of the economy—
small business, trade, farming—where the market approaches most closely the ideal free market. No one
who buys bread knows whether the wheat from which
it is made was grown by a Communist or a Republican, by a constitutionalist or a fascist, or, for that
matter, by a Negro or a white. This illustrates how an
impersonal market separates economic activities from
political views and protects men from being discrim-

inated against in their economic activities for reasons that are irrelevant to their productivity—whether these reasons are associated with their views or their color.

As this example suggests, the groups in our society that have the most at stake in the preservation and the strengthening of competitive capitalism are those minority groups which can most easily become the object of distrust and enmity of the majority—the Negroes, the Jews, the foreign born, to mention only the most obvious. Yet, paradoxically enough, the enemies of the free market—the socialists and Communists—have been recruited in disproportionate measure from these groups. Instead of recognizing that the existence of the market has protected them from the attitudes of their fellow countrymen, they mistakenly attribute the residual discrimination to the market.

Absolute freedom is impossible. Men's freedoms can conflict and when they do, one man's freedom must be limited to preserve another's. In addition, freedom is a tenable objective only for responsible individuals. We do not believe in unrestricted freedom for madmen or children; for them, paternalism is inescapable.

These qualifications on freedom as a sole and attainable objective make some departures in the direction of centralized control and paternalism both inevitable and desirable. The recognition of this fact should, however, be sharply distinguished from the superficially similar view that freedom is but one of a number of equally important objectives. It is one thing to recognize that anarchy is neither feasible nor desirable; that some restrictions on freedom are inevitable if the essence of freedom is to be preserved. It is quite another to regard such restrictions as desirable in their own right; to believe that it is appropriate to restrict the freedom of some adult individuals, not to protect the freedom of others but rather to protect these individuals themselves from "misusing" their freedom. This is the view that has been regaining ground in recent decades and that has led to the substitution of the ideal of a "mixed economy" for the ideal of a free economy.

The believer in freedom is doctrinaire about his principles. He should not be doctrinaire about specific proposals for intervention of the state in economic affairs. His principles themselves imply that some intervention is required to provide a stable legal and monetary framework for the market and to keep markets free by preventing private monopolies—whether of industry or labor—from themselves becoming a source of coercion. They imply also that some intervention may be required when market transactions have significant effects on individuals who are not parties to them, and on paternalistic grounds to protect the incompetent and to assure children an opportunity to have freedom when they mature.

The principles of the believer in freedom also imply, however, that in making up his balance sheet for any proposed intervention he must list among its liabilities that it encroaches on the market. Thereby the intervention both directly reduces the scope of freedom and indirectly threatens still further encroachment, by making it easier for enemies of freedom to gain control. The individualist can accept intervention as minor deviations from the general pattern but he should seek to have even these as general and impersonal as possible.

And, above all, the individualist should keep constantly in mind that the retention of a free market for the bulk of economic activity is an essential precondition for anything like a tolerable approximation to his ideal.

The Creative Powers
of a Free Civilization

Friedrich A. Hayek

Friedrich A. Hayek, 1974 Nobel laureate in economics, is presently working on his three-volume study of Law, Legislation and Liberty. *A native of Austria, his career as a teacher and scholar has taken him from Vienna to London, Freiburg, Salzburg and Chicago, where (from 1950 to 1962) he was professor of social and moral sciences and a member of the Committee on Social Thought at the University of Chicago. His many books include* The Constitution of Liberty *and* The Road to Serfdom.

The Socratic maxim that the recognition of our ignorance is the beginning of wisdom has profound
application to social life. If we are to comprehend how
society works we must first become aware, not merely
of our individual ignorance of most of the particular
circumstances which determine its actions, but also of
the necessary ignorance of man as such regarding much
or most that determines the course of his society.

It is no exaggeration to say that this unavoidable
ignorance of man concerning most of what affects his
own action is the most important single fact from which
any attempt to understand social life must start. This
is so because the advantages of social life, and particularly of those more advanced forms of social life which
we call civilization, rest on the paradox that the individual can use more knowledge than he possesses. It
might well be said that civilization begins where the individual can benefit from more knowledge than he can

himself acquire, and is able to cope with his ignorance by using knowledge which he does not possess.

Our ignorance, however, is by its very nature the most difficult subject to discuss. At first it might even seem by definition impossible to talk sense about it. We cannot discuss intelligently something about which we know nothing. We must at least be able to formulate the questions to which we do not know the answers. For this purpose we must possess some generic knowledge about the kind of thing, or the kind of world, we are talking about. If we are to understand how society works we must in this manner recognize at least the fact and the range of our ignorance. Though we cannot see in the dark, to understand our conduct we must at least be able to trace the limits of the dark areas.

The crucial facts come out clearly if we consider for a moment the significance both of the common assertion that man has created his civilization, and the conclusion often drawn that, since man has made his institutions, he can also change them as he pleases. This conclusion would be justified only if man had deliberately created civilization in full understanding of what he was doing, or if he at least fully comprehended how it was being maintained. In one sense it is, of course, true that man has made his civilization. It is the result of his actions, or rather of the actions of some hundreds of generations. But this does not mean that civilization is the product of human design, that man has aimed at what he produced, or even that he knows how it came to be what it is or on what its functioning and continued existence depend.

The whole conception that man, already endowed with a mind capable of conceiving civilization, set out to create that civilization as it was already preformed in his mind, is fundamentally false. Man does not simply impose upon nature a preformed mental pattern. His mind is itself a pattern constantly changing as a result of his endeavor to adapt himself to his surroundings. It is equally misleading to think that to achieve a higher civilization we have merely to put into effect the ideas now guiding us. If we are to advance there must be room for a continuous revision of our present conceptions and ideals as a result of further experience. We are as little able to conceive what civilization will be, or can be, five hundred or even fifty years hence as medieval man, or even our grandparents, were able to foresee our own manner of life.

The whole conception of man deliberately building his civilization stems from an erroneous intellectualism which treats human reason as something standing outside nature and possessed of knowledge or reasoning capacity independent of experience. But the growth of the human mind is part of the growth of civilization and it is the state of civilization at any moment that determines the scope and the possibilities of human values. The mind cannot foresee its own advance. Though we must always strive for the achievement of our present aims, we must also leave scope for new experiences and future events to decide which of those aims will be achieved. We must not go to the extreme position of some modern anthropologists when they argue "that it is not man who controls culture but the other way around." But it is certainly useful to be reminded that "it is only our profound and comprehensive ignorance of the nature of culture that makes it possible for us to believe that we direct and control it."[1] This view is at least a needed corrective of the intellectualist conception, a corrective that helps us to see more clearly the incessant interaction between our conscious intellectual striving for what our intellect pictures as achievable and the network of institutions, habits, and beliefs, within which something very different from what we have aimed at is produced.

To point the argument, let us for the moment disregard what has been our chief point so far, namely, how far man's mind is a product of the civilization in which he has grown up—and how little his conscious mind is aware of the experience which he actually employs, since it is embodied in the habits, conventions, language, and morals which are part of our makeup. Even so the magnitude of our individual ignorance of most of the circumstances that enable us to achieve our

---

[1] L. A. White, "Man's Control of Civilization: an Anthropomorphic Illusion," *Scientific Monthly*, 66, 1948, pp. 238–39.

aims is simply staggering, once we begin to reflect upon it.

Or, to put this differently: It is largely because civilization enables us constantly to profit from knowledge which we individually do not possess, and because each individual's use of his particular knowledge may serve to assist in the achievement of their ends by others unknown to him, that man as a member of civilized society can pursue his individual ends so much more successfully than he could alone. We know little of the particular facts to which the whole of social activity must continuously adjust itself in order to provide what we have learnt to expect. We know even less of the forces which bring about this adjustment by appropriately coordinating individual activity. Indeed, our attitude, when we discover how little we know of what makes us cooperate, is on the whole one of resentment rather than wonder or curiosity. Much of our occasional impetuous desire to smash the whole entangling machinery of civilization is due to this inability of man to understand what he is doing.

Civilization is built on the utilization of experience, acquired by countless individuals and generations and passed on through a process of communication and transmission of knowledge. The identification of the growth of civilization and the growth of knowledge which this suggests would be very misleading, however, if by "knowledge" we meant solely the conscious, explicit knowledge of individuals, the knowledge which means that we are able to state that this or that is so and so.[2] It would be still more misleading if knowledge were confined to scientific knowledge and it is important for the understanding of the further argument to remember that, contrary to a fashionable view,[3] scientific knowledge does not exhaust even all the explicit and conscious knowledge of which society makes constant use. The scientific methods of the search for knowledge are not suitable for satisfying all the needs for explicit knowledge on which the functioning of society is based.

Not all the knowledge of the ever changing particular facts, of the conditions of time and place of which man makes continuous use, lends itself to organization or centralized registration: much of it exists only dispersed among countless individuals. The same applies to that great part of expert knowledge which is not substantive knowledge but merely knowledge of where and how to find the needed information. I have discussed these different kinds of knowledge elsewhere, especially in an article in *Schweizer Monatshefte* (October 1956). But for our present purposes it is not this distinction between different kinds of rational

---

[2] See G. Ryle, "Knowing How and Knowing That," *Proceedings of the Aristotelian Society*, 1945–46.

[3] Compare the often quoted observation of F. P. Ramsay, *The Foundations of Mathematics* (Cambridge, 1925), p. 287: "There is nothing to know except science."

knowledge which is most important and we shall include all these different kinds when we speak of explicit knowledge.

The growth of knowledge and the growth of civilization are the same only if we interpret knowledge to
include all the human adaptations to environment in
which past experience has been incorporated. Not all
knowledge in this sense is part of our intellect and our
intellect is not the whole of our knowledge. Our habits
and skills, our emotional attitudes, our tools and our
institutions—all are in this sense more or less effective
adaptations formed by past experience, that have grown
up by selective elimination of less suitable conduct and
which are as much an indispensable foundation of successful action as is our conscious knowledge. Not all
these nonrational factors underlying our action are always conducive to success. Many of them may be retained long after they have outlived their usefulness and
even when they have become more an obstacle than a
help. Nevertheless, we could not do without them: even
successful employment of our intellect itself rests on
their constant use.

Man prides himself on the increase of his knowledge. But as a result of what he himself has created,
the limitations of his conscious knowledge and therefore the range of ignorance significant for his conscious
action have constantly increased. Ever since the beginning of modern science the best minds have recognized
"that the range of acknowledged ignorance will grow

with the advance of science."[4] Unfortunately, the popular effect of this scientific advance has been a belief, seemingly shared by many scientists, that the range of our ignorance is steadily diminishing and that we can therefore aim at more comprehensive and deliberate control of all human activities. Even more important is the fact that as civilization grows, individual man knows less and less about the man-made environment on which he more and more depends.

I have spoken of the transmission and communication of knowledge in order to point to two different aspects of the process of civilization. One is transmission in time, the handing on from generation to generation of an accumulated stock of knowledge. The other is communication among contemporaries of information on which they base their actions. These two aspects cannot be sharply separated, because the various means of communication between contemporaries are among the most important parts of the cultural heritage, of the transmitted tools which man, without understanding them, constantly uses in the pursuit of his ends.

This is familiar so far as it applies to the process of accumulation and transmission of that abstract, conscious knowledge which we call science, and also with regard to our awareness of the concrete features of the world in which we live—the "geography" of our sur-

---

[4] G. de Santillana, *The Crime of Galileo* (Chicago, 1955), p. 34.

roundings. But this is only a part, though the most conspicuous part, of the inherited stock of experience and it is the only part of which we necessarily "know," in the ordinary sense of the word. Yet we are better equipped to deal with our surroundings also because of the many "tools" other than conscious knowledge which we possess—tools the human race has evolved by a process of learning and handing on of the results. I stress the results here because the ever-better tools that have been passed on to successive generations embody only the results of experience without the whole of the experience being transmitted. Once the more efficient tool is available it will be used without the user knowing why it is better or even what the alternatives are.

In this sense the "tools" which man has evolved, and which are such an important part of his adaptation to his environment, do not consist solely of material implements, nor even of kinds of conduct that he individually uses as means for a purpose. Man is in a large measure ignorant not only of why he uses some tools rather than others, but also of what depends on his actions, of how far the results which he achieves are conditioned by conforming to habits of which he is unaware. This applies to civilized man not less but perhaps even more than to primitive man. With the growth of conscious knowledge there has been an equally important accumulation of tools in this wider sense, of tested and generally adopted ways of doing things. An advanced civilization and all the activities of civilized man, including his rational thought, depend as much on the unreflected use of these procedures as do the simplest kinds of human life.[5]

For the moment, however, we will consider not so much the knowledge thus handed down to us, as the manner in which *current* experience is utilized. This comprises, of course, the formation of new tools that can be used in the future; but above all it includes the help we get from the current experience of other people. Through this the dispersed knowledge and skill, and the varied habits and opportunities of all the members of society, combine in bringing about an adjustment of the activities of society to changing circumstances. So far as it is possible to separate these two aspects, current adjustment and change, we shall leave "progress" aside here and concentrate on those adjustments that must take place continuously merely to maintain civilization.

Every man who participates in civilization constantly benefits from current human experience which is not his own, and is led at the same time to take part in a

---

[5] In this connection compare the profound observation of A. N. Whitehead (*Introduction to Mathematics,* 1911, p. 61) that "civilization advances by extending the number of important operations which we can perform without thinking about them. Operations of thought are like cavalry charges in a battle—they are strictly limited in number, they require fresh horses, and must only be made at decisive moments."

process or adaptation to ever-changing circumstances of most of which he knows little. Yet in these changes the whole structure of society must share if it is to continue to exist. The persistence of an order through continuous change is based on a division and combination of knowledge among different persons, an aggregate of different sorts of knowledge the whole of which no single person can command.

Every change in conditions will make necessary some change in the use of resources, in the direction and kind of human activities, in habits and practices. And each change in the actions of those affected in the first instance will require further adjustments that will gradually extend through the whole of society. Every change thus in a sense creates a "problem" for society, even though no single individual perceives it as such; it is gradually "solved" by the establishment of a new overall adjustment. Those who take part in the process have little idea why they are doing what they do, and we have no way of predicting who will at each step first make the appropriate move or what particular combinations of knowledge and skill, personal attitudes and circumstances will suggest to some man the successful answer or by what channels his example will be transmitted to others who will follow the lead. It is difficult to conceive all the combinations of knowledge and skills which thus come into action, and from which arises the discovery of appropriate practices or devices that once found can be accepted generally. But the countless number of humble steps taken by anonymous persons, in the course of doing familiar things in changed circumstances, set the examples that prevail as the best after many have tried in their own way. They are as important as the major intellectual innovations which are explicitly recognized and communicated as such.

Who will prove to possess the right combination of aptitudes and opportunities to find the better way is just as little predictable as by what manner or process different kinds of knowledge and skill will combine to bring about solution of the problem. The successful combination of knowledge and aptitude does not, of course, normally result from people "putting their heads together"—from any process of thinking out in common the solution of their task. It results rather from imitation of what we have seen others do in similar circumstances and from an effort to improve upon their actions; from individual response to symbols or signs such as changes in prices or expressions of moral or esthetic esteem; from observing standards of conduct; in short, from using results of the experiences of others, past and present. The method by which only selected elements of relevant knowledge are brought to the different individuals who base their decisions upon them, rests on factors which as a whole are as little known to anybody as all the circumstances which can be communicated by them.

What is essential to the functioning of the process is that each individual is able to act on his particular knowledge, always unique at least so far as the knowledge of some particular circumstances is concerned; that he may use his individual skills and opportunities within the limits known to him and for his own individual purpose.

We have now reached the point at which the main contention of this essay should be readily intelligible. It is that the case for individual freedom rests largely on the recognition of the inevitable and universal ignorance of all of us concerning a great many of the factors on which the achievements of our ends and welfare depend.

If there were omniscient men, if we could know not only all that affects the attainment of our present wishes but also all our future wants and desires, then there would be little case for liberty—while liberty of the individual, in turn, would of course make complete foresight impossible. Liberty is essential in order to leave room for the unforeseeable and unpredictable: we want it because we have learnt to expect from it the opportunity of realizing many of our aims. It is because every individual knows so little, and in particular because we rarely know which of us knows best, that we trust the independent and competitive efforts of many to induce the emergence of what we shall want when we see it.

Humiliating to human pride as the insight may be, we must recognize that we owe the advance and even the preservation of civilization to a maximum of opportunity for accidents to happen. These accidents occur in the combination of knowledge and attitudes, skills and habits acquired by individual men, and also in the confrontation of qualified men with the particular circumstances with which they are equipped to deal. Our necessary ignorance of so much means that we have to deal largely with probabilities and chances.

Of course, it is true of social as of individual life that favorable accidents usually do not just happen. We must prepare for them. But still they remain chances and do not become certainties. They involve risks deliberately taken, the misfortunes of individuals and groups who are as meritorious as others who prosper, the possibility of serious failure or relapse even for the majority, and merely a high probability of a net gain on balance. All we can do is to heighten the chance that some special constellation of individual equipment and circumstance will result in the shaping of some new tool (in the wide sense in which we have used the word) or the improvement of an old one, and increase the prospect that such innovations will become rapidly known to those who can take advantage of them.

Man learns by the disappointment of expectations. Of course we should not add elements of unpredictability by foolish human institutions, in which case the stultification of our efforts would teach us nothing significant. We should, rather, improve human institutions with the aim of increasing the possibility of correct foresight. But we should above all provide the maximum of opportunity for unknown individuals to learn facts of which we are yet unaware and opportunity to use this knowledge in their actions. For the achievement of our ends depends on forces which we do not know in detail and whose operation we understand only to a small degree.

It is in the utilization, in the mutually adjusted efforts of different people, of more knowledge than anyone possesses or than it is possible intellectually to synthetize, that achievements emerge that are greater than any one man's mind can foresee. We sometimes forget that freedom means the renunciation of direct control of individual efforts and the limitation of coercion to the enforcement of abstract rules. It is because of this renunciation of the use of coercion for the achievement of specific ends that a free society can make use of so much more knowledge than the mind of any ruler can comprehend.

From this foundation of the argument for liberty it follows that we shall not achieve its ends if we confine liberty to the particular instances where we know it will do good. Freedom granted only where it can be known beforehand that its effects will be beneficial would not be freedom. If we knew how freedom would be used, the case for it would largely disappear. We could then achieve the same result by telling people to do what freedom would enable them to do. But we shall never get the benefits of freedom, never obtain those unforeseeable new developments for which it provides the opportunity, if it is not granted also where the uses made of it by some do not seem desirable. It is therefore no argument against individual freedom that it is frequently abused or used for ends that are recognized as socially undesirable. Our faith in freedom rests not on demonstrable results in particular circumstances, but on the belief that it will on balance release more' forces for the good than for the bad.

It also follows that the importance of freedom to do particular things has nothing to do with the question of whether we or the majority are ever likely to make use of that particular possibility. To grant no more freedom than all can exercise would be completely to misconceive its function. The freedom that will be used by only one man in a million may be more important to society and more beneficial to the majority than any freedom we all use.[6]

Indeed, it might almost be said that freedom to do a

---

[6] H. Rashdall, "The Philosophical Theory of Property," *Property, Its Rights and Duties* (New York and London, 1915), p. 62: "The plea for liberty is not sufficiently met by insisting, as has been so eloquently and humorously done by Mr. Lowes Dickinson (*Justice and Liberty: a Political Dialogue,* 1908, *e.g.* pp. 129, 131), upon the absurdity of supposing that the propertyless laborer under the ordinary capitalistic regime enjoys any liberty of which socialism would deprive him. For it may be of extreme importance that *some* should enjoy liberty— that it should be possible for some few men to be able to dispose of their time in their own way—although such liberty may be neither possible nor desirable for the great majority. That culture requires a considerable differentiation in social conditions is also a principle of unquestionable importance."

particular thing is the more precious for society as a whole the less likely the opportunity for its use. The less likely it is that the opportunity will occur, the more unlikely also that the experience to be gained will be recovered if such a nearly unique chance is missed. It is also probably true that the majority is not directly interested in most of the things it is most important that we should be free to do. If it were otherwise, the results of freedom could also be achieved by the majority deciding what should be done by the individuals. But majority action is of necessity confined to the already tried and ascertained, to issues on which agreement has already been reached in that process of discussion that must be preceded by different experiences and actions on the part of the different individuals.

The benefits I derive from freedom are thus largely the result of the uses of freedom by others, and mostly of uses of freedom that I myself could never make. It is therefore not merely and not even mainly the freedom which I can exercise myself which is important for me. It may even be that in many ways freedom for others is more important for us than freedom for ourselves, and it is certainly more important that anything can be tried by somebody than that all can do the same things. It is not because we like to be able to do particular things, not because we regard any particular freedom as essential to our happiness, that we have a claim to freedom. The instinct that makes us revolt against any physical restraint, though a helpful ally, is not always a safe guide for justifying or delimiting freedom. What is important is not what freedom I personally would like to exercise but what freedom some odd person may need in order to do things beneficial to society, a freedom we can assure to this unknown single person only by giving it to all.

The benefits of freedom are therefore not confined to the free—or it is at least not by those aspects of freedom that each man himself uses that he mainly benefits. There can be no doubt that in history unfree majorities have benefited from the existence of free minorities, and that today unfree societies benefit and even maintain their cultural level by what they obtain and learn from free societies. Of course, the benefits we derive from the freedom of others are greater as the number of those who can exercise freedom increases. The argument for the freedom of some therefore applies to the freedom of all. But it is still better for all that some should be free than none, or that more should be free than fewer. The point to recognize is that the importance of the freedom to do a particular thing has nothing to do with the number of people who want to do it; it might almost be said to be in inverse proportion. One lesson we must draw from these considerations is that a society may be hamstrung by controls although the great majority may not be aware that their freedom is significantly curtailed. If we proceeded on the assumption that only the freedoms the majority will exercise are important we would be certain to create a stagnant society with all the characteristics of unfreedom.

The undesigned "new" factors that constantly emerge in the process of adaptation consist in the first instance of new arrangements or patterns in which the efforts of different individuals are coordinated, and of new constellations in the use of our resources, which are in their nature as temporary as the changed conditions that have evoked them. There will, also, be modifications of tools and institutions adapted to the new circumstances. Some of these will be purely temporary adaptations to the conditions of the moment, while others will prove to be improvements, increasing the versatility of the existing tools and usages, and will therefore be retained. They constitute a better adaptation not merely to the particular circumstances of time and place but to some permanent feature of our environment. In such spontaneous "formations"[7] is embodied a perception of the general laws that govern nature. Parallel with this cumulative embodiment of experience in tools and forms of action will go a growth

---

[7] For the use of this term, more appropriate in this connection than the usual "institutions," see my study on *The Counter-Revolution of Science,* 1952, p. 83.

of explicit knowledge, of formulated generic rules that can be communicated by language from person to person.

This process by which the new emerges is relatively best known and most readily comprehensible—though still inadequately appreciated—in the intellectual sphere where the results are new ideas. It is the field in which most people are aware at least of some of the individual steps of the process, where we necessarily know of what is happening and where the necessity of freedom is consequently fairly generally understood. Most scientists realize that we cannot plan the advance of knowledge, that in the voyage into the unknown which the enterprise of research always is, we are in great measure dependent on the vagaries of individual genius and of circumstances, and that, though a new idea will spring up in a single mind, it will be the result of a combination of concepts, habits, and circumstances brought to one person by society, the result of lucky accidents as much as of systematic effort.

Because we are necessarily aware that our advances in the intellectual sphere spring often from the unforeseen and undesigned, we tend to overstress the relative importance of freedom in this field compared with the importance of the freedom of *doing* things. But the freedom of research and belief, and of speech and discussion, the importance of which most people recognize, refers only to the last stage of the process in which new truths are discovered. It would be like treating the crowning part of an edifice as the whole of it if we were to extol the value of intellectual liberty at the expense of the value of the liberty of doing things. If we have new ideas to discuss, different views to adjust, it is because these ideas and views arise from the efforts of individuals in ever-new circumstances, availing themselves in their concrete tasks of the new tools and forms of action of which they have learnt. The intellectualist view that stresses exclusively the formation of abstract and generic ideas is a consequence of the fact that this part of the process of the advance of knowledge is the most obvious and the one with which those who think about its nature are most familiar and in which they have a special interest.

The nonintellectual part of the same process, the formation of the changed material environment in which the new emerges, requires for its understanding and appreciation a much greater effort of imagination. We may sometimes be able to reconstruct the intellectual processes that have led to a new idea, but we can scarcely ever hope to reconstruct the sequence and combination of the contributions that did not consist in the acquisition of new explicit knowledge—all the favorable habits and skills employed, the facilities and opportunities used, and the particular environment of the main actors that has brought about the result. Our efforts toward understanding that part of the process can go little further than showing on simplified models the kind of forces that are at work, the general principle rather than the specific character of the influences that operate.[8] In the nature of the thing each man can always be concerned only with what he does know. Therefore, those features which, while the process is under way, are not consciously known to anybody, are commonly disregarded and can perhaps never be traced in detail.

In fact, these unconscious features not only are commonly disregarded but are often treated as if they were a hindrance rather than a help or an essential condition. Because they are not "rational" in the sense of explicitly entering into our process of reasoning, they are often treated as irrational in the sense of being contrary to intelligent action. Yet, though much of the nonrational that affects our action may also be in this sense irrational, many of the "mere habits" and "meaningless institutions" that we unquestioningly use and presuppose in our actions are essential conditions for what we achieve, successful adaptations of society that are constantly improved and on which the range of what we can achieve depends. While it is important to discover their defects, we could not for a moment go on without constantly relying on them.

The manner in which we have learnt to order our day, to dress, to eat, and arrange our houses, to speak, write, and use the countless tools and implements of

---

[8] Compare my article on "Degrees of Explanation," *British Journal for the Philosophy of Science,* November 1955.

civilization, no less than the "know-how" used in production and trade, all furnish us constantly with the foundations on which our own contributions to the process of civilization must be based. And it is in the new use and improvement of whatever the facilities of civilization offer to us that the new ideas arise which are ultimately handled in the intellectual sphere. Though the conscious manipulation of abstract thought, once it has been set in train, has in some measure a life of its own, it would not long continue and develop without the constant challenges that do not originate in the intellectual sphere but which arise from the ability of people to act in a new manner, trying new ways of doing things and altering the whole structure of civilization in adaptation to change. The intellectual process is in effect only a process of elaboration, selection, and elimination of conscious ideas already formed. But the flow of new ideas to a great extent surges up from the sphere in which action, often nonrational action, and material events impinge upon each other. It would dry up if freedom were confined to the intellectual sphere.

Thus, the importance of freedom does not depend on the elevated character of the activities that it makes possible. Freedom of action, even action in humble things, is as important as freedom of thought and freedom of belief. It has become a common practice to disparage liberty of action by calling it "economic liberty." But not only is the concept of liberty of action much wider than that of the economic liberty which it includes; what is more important, it is very questionable whether actions which can be called purely economic exist in this sense, and whether any restrictions on liberty can be confined to what are called merely economic aspects. Economic considerations are merely the process by which we endeavor to reconcile and adjust our different purposes, which in the last resort are all not economic (or nearly all: excepting only those of the miser or the man to whom making money has become an end in itself).

Most of what has been said so far applies not only to man's use of the means for the achievement of his ends but also to these ends themselves. It is one of the essential characteristics of a free society that its goals are open, that new ends of conscious effort can spring up, first with a few individuals or a small minority, to become in time the ends of all or most.

We must recognize that even what we regard as good or beautiful is changeable, if not in any recognizable manner that could entitle us to take any kind of relativist position, yet in the sense that in many ways we do not know what will appear as good or beautiful to another generation; we do not know why we regard this or that as good, or who is right when people differ on whether something is good or not. It is not only in his knowledge, but also in his aims and values, that man is the creature of the process of civilization, and in the last resort it is the significance of these individual wishes for the perpetuation of the group or the species that will determine whether they will persist or change. It is of course a mistake to believe that we can draw conclusions about what our values ought to be, because we realize that they are a product of evolution. But we cannot reasonably doubt that these values are created and altered by the same evolutionary forces that have produced our intelligence. All that we can know is that the ultimate decision about what is accepted as right and wrong will be made not by individual human wisdom but by the disappearance of the groups that have adhered to the "wrong" beliefs.

It is in the pursuit of man's aims of the moment that all the devices of civilization have to prove themselves; that the ineffective is discarded and the efficient handed on. But there is more to it than the fact that new ends constantly arise with the satisfaction of old needs and with the appearance of new opportunities. Which individuals, and which groups, succeed and continue to exist depends as much on the goals which they pursue, the values that govern their action, as on the tools and capacities at their command. A group may prosper or be extinguished just as much because of the ethical code it obeys, or because of the ideals of beauty or well-being that guide it, as because of the degree to which it has learned or not learned to satisfy its material needs. Within any given society particular groups may rise or sink because of the ends they pursue and the standards of conduct which they observe. And the ends of the successful group will tend to become the ends of all members of the society.

At most we understand only partially why the values we hold, or the ethical rules we observe, are conducive to the continued existence of our society. Nor, under continuously changing conditions, can we be sure that all the rules that have proved themselves as conducive to that purpose will remain so. Though there is a presumption that any established social standard contributes in some manner to the preservation of a civilization, our only way of knowing this is to ascertain whether it continues to prove itself in competition with other standards tried by other individuals or groups.

The competition, on which the process of selection rests, must be understood in the widest sense of the term. It is as much a competition between organized and unorganized groups as a competition among individuals. To think of the process in contrast to co-operation or organization would be to misconceive its nature. The endeavor to achieve specific results by cooperation and organization is as much a part of competition as are individual efforts, and successful group relations also prove their efficiency in competition between groups organized on different principles. The distinction relevant here is not between individual and group action but between arrangements in which alternative ways based on different views and habits may be tried, and on the other hand, arrangements in which one agency has the exclusive rights and the power to coerce others to keep out of the field. It is only when such exclusive rights are granted, on the presumption of superior knowledge of particular individuals or groups, that the process ceases to be experimental and the beliefs that happen to be prevalent at the moment tend to become a main obstacle to the advancement of knowledge.

Thus the argument for liberty is not an argument against organization, which is one of the most powerful tools human reason can employ, but an argument against all exclusive, privileged, monopolistic organization, against the use of coercion to prevent others from doing better. Every organization is based on given knowledge, and even an organization designed to increase knowledge can be effective only insofar as the knowledge and beliefs on which the design of the organization rests are correct. Insofar as any facts not yet known contradict the beliefs on which the structure of the organization is based, this can show itself only in its failure and supersession by a different type of organization. Organization is likely to be beneficial and effective so long as it is voluntary and is embedded in a free sphere, either adjusting itself to circumstances not taken into account in its conception, or failing. To turn the whole of society into a single organization built and directed according to a single plan would be to extinguish the forces that have formed the very reason that planned it.

It is worth a moment's reflection as to what would happen if only what was agreed upon to be the best knowledge of society were to be used in any action. If all attempts that seemed wasteful in the light of the now generally accepted knowledge were prohibited and only such questions asked, or such experiments tried, as seemed significant in the light of ruling opinion. Mankind might then well reach a point where its knowledge allowed it adequately to predict the consequences of all conventional actions and where no disappointment or failure would occur. Man would seem to have subjected his surroundings to his reason because nothing of which he could not predict the results would be done. We might conceive of a civilization thus coming to a standstill, not because the possibilities of further growth had been exhausted, but because man had succeeded in so completely subjecting all his actions and his immediate surroundings to his existing state of knowledge that no occasion would arise for new knowledge to appear.

The rationalist who desires to subject everything to human reason is faced with a real dilemma. The use of reason aims at control and predictability. But the process of the advance of reason rests on freedom and the unpredictability of human action. Those who extol the powers of human reason usually see only one side of that intermingling of thought and action in which reason is at the same time used and formed. They do not see that for advancement the social process from which the advances of reason emerge must remain free from its control!

There can be little doubt that man owes some of his greatest successes in the past to the fact that he has *not* been able to control social life. His continued success may well depend on his deliberately refraining from exercising controls now in his power. In the past, the spontaneous forces of growth, however much restricted, usually asserted themselves even against the organized coercion of the state. With the technological means of control now at the disposal of government it is no longer certain that this assertion is possible; soon, at least, it may be impossible.

The necessity of cultivating individual freedom as a deliberate aim of policy, rather than treating it as something that has to be tolerated because it cannot be prevented, has become greater than ever. We are not far from the point at which the deliberately organized forces of society may snuff out those spontaneous forces on which all advance depends.

Individuality in American History

Arthur A. Ekirch, Jr.

Arthur A. Ekirch, Jr., is professor of history at the State University of New York, Albany. He was educated at Dartmouth College and Columbia University, and was a Guggenheim Fellow in 1953–54. Among his many books are The Decline of American Liberalism *and* The Civilian and the Military.

The historian, together with other students of modern society, cannot fail to be impressed with the strength of the worldwide pressures working against freedom for the individual. Yet he is also constantly reminded, perhaps more than others, that individuality has been one of the historic characteristics of human nature in general and of the American personality in particular. Though much weakened in recent decades, individualism has played a major role in American life. This fact alone would seem to suggest caution before we relegate it to the scrap heap of discarded or outmoded ideas.

Like other important attributes of our character and civilization, individuality or individualism is an outgrowth of many forces. More specifically, and rather obviously, it is a product of inheritance and environment—the experience of Europe and the hope of America. It is, of course, beyond the scope of this paper, or the ability of its author, to trace through all history the conflict between the demands of society and the urgings of individuality. Something of this conflict has probably always affected human personality, but individuality as it has developed in the United States goes back most directly to English history and experience.

Among the legacies handed down from Britain to the American colonies was recognition of the importance of political and religious freedom for the individual. The English people had come to pride themselves on their love of liberty and hostility to arbitrary power. Essential to the English political tradition was the belief that individuals had certain natural rights which no government could violate with impunity. This tradition, reinforced by the revolutions of the seventeenth century, was most eloquently expressed in the writings of John Locke. This philosopher of the "Glorious Revolution" of 1688, also espoused a policy of religious toleration; and the natural rights and privileges of the individual, political and religious, though imperfectly respected in the mother country, were considered a part of the person of the Englishman, to be taken wherever he went. These rights accordingly were included in the charters granted to the American colonies by Great Britain.

In the new American colonial environment, the struggle to subdue the untamed wilderness, and the opportunities held out at the same time by a seemingly limitless western frontier, were both a stimulus and a potential reward to individual enterprise. An abundance of free, or near-free, soil offered unique economic advantages, and European feudal customs of restricted land tenure proved impossible to maintain in the New World. The great natural resources and wealth of America encouraged not only economic individualism or *laissez faire,* but provided also an atmosphere friendly to political and religious liberty. Thus American individualism, rooted in the philosophy of natural rights and expressed in the concepts of limited government and religious toleration, was amply reinforced by the ever-widening opportunities of day-to-day life in the New World.

Born in the Old World, but nurtured in the New, individualism was an essential feature in the growth of American democracy. On the whole, the colonial period was one of progress toward democracy along individualist lines, and in the American revolution patriots stressed the negative side of government, seeking emancipation from British restrictions on trade and commerce. The Declaration of Independence appealed to the rights of man, while the new state constitutions with their bills of rights put into practical application the philosophy of the Declaration. "In every instance in these early state constitutions," as J. B. MacMaster wrote,

> The state is presented as created by the people, and existing solely for the good of the individual. Its sole duty is stated to be to protect him in the full enjoyment of his natural and inalienable rights. Public officials are declared to

be the trustees of the people; the right of revolution is inherent in society. In no instance is the state presented as the provider of office, the creator of monopolies.

The federal Constitution, drafted in 1787, was an example of the postrevolutionary trend away from eighteenth-century individualism toward greater centralization and concentration of power in the hands of government. But the Constitution also set forth the framework of limited government with its separation of powers and with the addition later of the Bill of Rights. While such a system of checks and balances reflected a distrust of popular democracy, it also served to guard against the danger of tyranny or the assumption of despotic authority. In the new national government, both Hamiltonian Federalists and Jeffersonian Republicans subscribed to the theory of the natural rights of the individual, but it was Jefferson who was the great exemplar of individuality in his political philosophy. According to the Jeffersonian agrarian view of society, property widely diffused and devoted largely to agricultural pursuits, gave the type of security to the individual which formed the very basis of democratic government.

Jefferson's emphasis upon the self-sufficient individual, living in a self-contained community with widespread ownership of land and commensurate economic advantages, was justified by the New England town as well as by the American frontier. But within Jefferson's own lifetime the American environment, originally so

well suited to individualism, underwent a partial transformation. Negro slavery, with its denial of full individuality in the human personality, became more
tightly fastened upon the South. Then, immediately
after the War of 1812, and even more in the Jacksonian
era, old agrarian ideals began to suffer the competition
of new concentrations of wealth, power, and population. A commercial and manfacturing aristocracy vied
for supremacy with the enfranchised urban masses,
while the frontier spirit became identified with a crude
conception of manifest destiny, in which the rights of
Indians, Mexicans, and others were brushed aside.

Although the industrial revolution had not yet entered its main phase in the United States in the period
before the Civil War, transcendentalists and romantics
in assaying its effects already foresaw the dire consequences of the factory system for their prized individuality and Emersonian self-reliance. Thoreau's
protest against industrialism was, of course, the most
thoroughgoing. The author of *Walden* and of *Civil Dis-
obedience* summed up his feelings when he complained
bitterly of the approaching day when huckleberries
would have to be purchased in a store instead of being
picked at will from the fields. "I suspect," he wrote in
his *Journal* for August 6, 1858,

> that the inhabitants of England and of the Continent of
> Europe have thus lost their natural rights with the increase
> of population and of monopolies. The wild fruits of the
> earth disappear before civilization, or are only to be found

in large markets. The whole country becomes, as it were, a town or beaten common, and the fruits left are a few hips and haws.

In the decades before the Civil War, American political democracy was already beginning to diverge from the individualist tenets of Jefferson and other eighteenth-century philosopher statesmen. Under Andrew Jackson, democracy was equated with majority rule, while individuals and minorities were faced with the loss of time-honored natural rights. The issue, as Alexis de Tocqueville clearly pointed out, was not the denial of majority rule, but rather a concern lest the majority fail to protect the rights of minorities and individuals. Fearing that if ever free institutions were destroyed in the United States it would be by the tyranny of the majority, Tocqueville declared: "I know of no country in which there is so little independence of mind and real freedom of discussion as in America."[1]

Distinguishing between freedom for the individual and the American stress upon equality, Tocqueville observed that the love of equality and hatred of privileges, even the slightest, lead to the demand that all rights and privileges be concentrated in the hands of the government. These are then dispensed to the citizenry as a matter of governmental favor or largesse. A strong central government requires uniformity and equality at the expense of individuality and dissent.

---

[1] Alexis de Tocqueville, *Democracy in America,* ed. Phillips Bradley (New York: Knopf, 1945), I, pp. 263f.

While this might contribute to such social and collective undertakings as war, it could also lead to a type of popular servitude in which the "will of man is not shattered, but softened, bent, and guided. . . ."

> The more equal the conditions of men become and the less strong men individually are, the more easily they give way to the current of the multitude and the more difficult it is for them to adhere by themselves to an opinion which the multitude discard. . . .
>
> As the conditions of men become equal among a people, individuals seem of less and society of greater importance; or rather every citizen, being assimilated to all the rest, is lost in the crowd, and nothing stands conspicuous but the great and imposing image of the people at large. This naturally gives the men of democratic periods a lofty opinion of the privileges of society and a very humble notion of the rights of individuals. . . .[2]

Since the time of the Civil War, the traditional individuality of the American character has come more and more into question. While this decline of individualism has frequently been deplored, it has even more frequently been regarded as inevitable. For the United States, as well as for Europe, John Stuart Mill's classic paean to individual liberty came at a time when, in the words of his latest biographer, "The era of the beehive state was dawning, and the freedom of the individual was going out of fashion."[3] According to

---

[2] *Ibid.*, II, pp. 114, 290, 295, 319.

[3] Michael St. John Packe, *The Life of John Stuart Mill* (New York: Macmillan, 1954), p. 403.

Mill, the threat to individualist liberalism and democracy was coming "not, as Marx was to insist, by economic forces which made it illusory, but by mass opinion and bureaucracy."

In the United States, the years following the Civil War were characterized by a tremendous economic surge that swept away the last frontiers of the Far West and carried American industry to levels of production surpassing all the rest of the world. In the course of this expansion, individuality in its crudest forms was at first strengthened. The Indian fighters, gold miners, cowboys, and frontier desperadoes were certainly individualists, often callous to the point of violence in ignoring the rights of their fellow men. In similar fashion, the so-called robber barons were ruthless and rugged individualists who carried out business consolidations which eliminated the competition of rivals.

But this individualism of exploitation and consolidation was not in harmony with the older philosophy of natural rights and limited government. No matter how much the farmer or manufacturer talked of *laissez faire,* in practice each sought the protection of a paternalistic government that offered direct subsidies in the form of tariffs and land grants. More significant still, the swift exploitation of the West and the rapid growth of American industry and population, though piling up stores of material goods, also hastened the advent of the mass man and society of the twentieth century. The immigrant population coming to America from Europe easily succumbed to control by public opinion, and by the political bureaucracy.

Although most Americans, caught up in the mounting enthusiasm for civil service reform, were inclined to dismiss what E. L. Godkin in 1882 called "The Danger of an Office-Holding Aristocracy," the United States like Europe was moving in that direction. Max Weber, who later was to compose a classic study of bureaucracy, was stimulated in his thinking by a visit to the United States in 1904. Here Weber perceived the paradox of the democracy of the country expressed in the bureaucratic machines which dominated political parties as well as municipal, state, and federal governments. Weber identified bureaucracy with rationality and rationality, in turn, with mechanization, depersonalization, and routinization—all of which were at odds with personal freedom and with democracy in an individualist sense. Whether in Germany, Russia, or the United States, Weber believed the outlook for individualist democracy was dark.

> . . . Everywhere the house is ready-made for a new servitude. It only waits for the tempo of technical economic "progress" to slow down and for rent to triumph over profit. The latter victory, joined with the exhaustion of the remaining free soil and free market, will make the masses "docile."[4]

---

[4] H. M. Gerth and C. Wright Mills, *From Max Weber: Essays in Sociology* (New York: Oxford, 1946), pp. 17–18, 49–50, 71–72.

The United States was not a complete bureaucracy when Weber wrote at the turn of the century, but it was tending in that direction, developing the power of the bureaucracy by permanence and pensions, by the arrogance of the expert *vis-à-vis* legislatures and elected officials, and by the vogue of specialized or jargonized knowledge tested through examinations. In the early twentieth century, the individual was approaching anonymity, squeezed between the closing frontier and the expanding powers of the political state and a machine society.

Although some mourned the loss of liberties which they associated with an older, frontier, agrarian tradition, nevertheless the impact of war reinforced the antiindividualistic effects of an industrial society. World War I, verging upon the later climax of total war, immensely stimulated the role of the government as against the individual citizen. The government regulation demanded by "progressives" in the 1900s, as a part of a program of reform, was achieved after 1917 in connection with a war economy. Regulation in the sense of trying to restore a competitive individualism now frankly yielded to regulation to achieve economic integration and greater industrial efficiency. The war made partners of government and business, and the individual caught up in the rising tide of nationalism and patriotism could offer only feeble protest.

War, as it was carried on in the years from 1914 to 1918, was a compulsory business from beginning to end. Herbert Spencer's old distinction between a military and an industrial society vanished in the prosecution of modern total war, and the individual, whether at home or in the army, lost his individuality to the dictates of the state.

> All the activities of society are linked together as fast as possible to this central purpose of making a military offensive or a military defense, and the State becomes what in peace times it has vainly struggled to become—the inexorable arbiter and determinant of men's businesses and attitudes and opinions. The slack is taken up, the cross-currents fade out, and the nation moves lumberingly and slowly, but with ever accelerated speed and integration, towards the great end, towards that "peacefulness of being at war . . ."

To Randolph Bourne, writing the above in his *Untimely Papers* (1919), war was the health of the state. But, while it emphasized mass conformity and the herd instinct, Bourne sorrowfully saw that it also gave classes and individuals a lift from the ordinary routine of life, in which they were able to approximate to themselves the ideals of the state and the virtues of the whole:

> At war, the individual becomes almost identical with his society. He achieves a superb self-assurance, an intuition of the rightness of all his ideas and emotions, so that in the suppression of opponents or heretics he is invincibly strong; he feels behind him all the power of the collective community.

Evincing a mild surprise at the docility of his fellow Americans, Henry Adams described their wartime temper. "As far as I know," he wrote to Charles M. Gaskell in June 1917, "we have behaved like lambs and done everything we were told to do. Never could I have conceived that in a short three months we could have gone into a great war and adopted a conscription not unworthy of Germany, at the bidding of a President who was elected only a few months ago on the express ground that he had kept us at peace." Liberals, carried away in the intensity of waging war, or seduced by the charm of being "big shots" in Washington, or later at Versailles, were helping to prepare the way for the disillusionment that followed the Armistice.

The postwar revolt of the twenties reflected the frustration of the individual beset by the pressures of a business civilization and a paternalistic state. Although wartime government regulation of economic life was partially relaxed, demobilization in the sense of intellectual freedom was hardly achieved. The private lives of individuals were subjected as never before to state interference. Prohibition was only the most obvious of the censorious laws that regimented individual customs and morals, and even the books the individual might read or the moving pictures he might see. Individualism, carried to the point of any radical criticism of postwar society, was suppressed in a wave of conservative reaction. Meanwhile, there were new dangers in the growing national tendency to equate democracy with majority will and with equality in the material comforts supplied by technology. Pressures to conform and keep up a higher standard of living were impairing the psychological balance and level of quality and competence of man as an individual.

At the height of the prosperity of the 1920s, discerning critics questioned its cost in terms of human values. James Truslow Adams condemned the materialism and standardization of *Our Business Civilization.* Prosperity, he wrote, entailed too high a price in goods and services. The resulting clamor and competition for piling up material *things* was harmful to intellectual life and ethical values. In still more critical fashion, Ralph Borsodi indicted the twenties as "ugly." The idea that man's welfare or comfort was dependent on an unending increase in production was destroying the resources of the earth and the time man would have to enjoy them. The factory system, he argued, would drive industrialized nations to socialization of production and consumption, and at the same time destroy individuality in the quest for a mass-minded equality and conformity.

These attacks on industrialism, at the very climax of its seeming success in the twenties, were indications that material prosperity had somehow failed to satisfy basic human and individual needs. Borsodi's plea for decentralization was in line with the wishes of others for a new humanism, or for a return to Jeffersonian agrarian principles. This last desire was emphasized in 1930 in a celebrated manifesto signed by twelve prominent southern writers and teachers who indicted industrialism for its effect on man and the arts. Increased production, they asserted, led only to a useless consumption and leisure devoid of happiness or meaning.[5]

Skeptical of much of this traditional individualism because it was so often a very limited affair, confined to an aristocracy of upper and middle classes, John Dewey in 1930 published his *Individualism Old and New*.

Dewey was not unmindful of, nor enthusiastic about, the way in which American civilization had come to emphasize mass production and mass consumption. Under the pressures of advertising, buying became a duty while the older virtue of thrift was relegated to an age of individualism. In discussing the plight of the "lost Individual," Dewey pointed out that the loyalties which once gave the individual focus and direction had disappeared. The individual in consequence was bewildered, and rendered still more insecure, by the mounting specter of technological unemployment. Opposed to the rise of totalitarian nationalisms, but hopeful that individualism could somehow be recreated in a public or democratic socialism that would not enhance the il-

---

[5] Twelve Southerners, *I'll Take My Stand* (New York: Harper & Bros.), pp. ix-xx (Introduction).

liberal pressure of statism, Dewey concluded that "the solution of the crisis in culture is identical with the recovery of composed, effective, and creative individuality."

Dewey's argument for a "new" individualism found a ready response in the years immediately following. Impelled by the depression to reexamine the state of civilization and society, writers and politicians placed the older American individualism under heavy attack. The human misery caused by hard times obviously required large measures of social cooperation and mutual aid. Private and local facilities seemed hopelessly inadequate to meet the emergency, and the consequent growing dependence on government intervention afforded still further basis for the denunciation of individualism.

That the economic crisis was in many ways a result of unbridled nationalism and industrialism was forgotten in the rush toward a new political and economic collectivism. Tying American individualism to the pioneer ways of an older frontier civilization, Dean Guy Stanton Ford of the University of Minnesota saw such a society outmoded by science and invention, by the factory and the city. "The result of science is to illustrate, emphasize, and increase the interdependence of men and nations. . . . Science is not interested in individuals. . . . If our democratic craft is water-logged with the individualism, localism, and the *laissez faire* suitable to that bygone day will it reach port in safety?" Dean Ford asked.[6]

Alfred North Whitehead, the distinguished philosopher, in his *Adventures of Ideas* related modern big-business industrialism to feudalism by virtue of its interlocking nature. Individualists and socialists debated over what were merely details, while "The self-sufficing independent man, with his peculiar property which concerns no one else, is a concept without any validity for modern civilization."

In the chaos and suffering of the depression, concern over the fate of the free individual was submerged in the bitterness of the masses. The very number of individuals affected by the economic crisis deprived them of consideration as individuals. In the past, freedom had meant individual liberty and respect for minority rights; now the new freedom preached in Europe and America was the right of the desperate majority against the individual. Herbert Hoover's assertion that the fundamental issue facing the American people was the worldwide attack on individual liberty was dismissed as a reactionary view. In its haste to control the forces unloosed by total war and modern technology, Hoover believed that mankind stood ready to sacrifice both the intellectual and the economic freedoms on which political liberty is based. Though agree-

[6] Guy Stanton Ford, *Science and Civilization* (Minneapolis: University of Minnesota Press, 1933), pp. 14, 23.

ing with Hoover's strictures upon the New Deal, Supreme Court Justice Harlan Fiske Stone felt that the depression and the complexity of modern industrial society prevented any return to individualism in its more traditional meaning. He therefore urged the former President not to publish his criticism.[7]

Throughout the civilized world, under the impact of the depression, there was a headlong flight from the concept of freedom. The so-called "revolt of the masses" was actually more a tragic popular affirmation of willingness to accept the "security" allegedly offered by variant forms of state socialism. In Europe, the despair of the masses, rather than their revolt, was the key to an understanding of fascism. In the United States, where it was still possible to avoid the worse excesses of statism, the New Deal nevertheless placed its major emphasis upon a type of liberty that minimized individual freedom in favor of a greater social security and economic equality of the whole. "Talk of liberty in reform circles now was likely to produce a yawn, if not a scowl; opportunity, at least opportunity for the millions to have jobs, was the point."[8]

Collectivism of one sort or another was more widespread than ever before in modern history, but though

---

[7] Hoover-Stone correspondence, cited in A. T. Mason, *Security Through Freedom* (Ithaca: Cornell University Press, 1955), pp. 74ff.

[8] Eric Goldman, *Rendezvous with Destiny* (New York: Knopf, 1952), p. 329.

the collective life had indeed arrived, "and with it a concentration of authority that was impossible in the heyday of individualism," this authority still had to be exercised by individuals, whether as dictators, demagogues, or democratic statesmen. Instead of suppressing the predatory individual, the collective national state might, in the words of Barbara S. Morgan, "merely shift his main activities to the political field and place more destinies in his hands." Despite the popular dismissal of rugged individualism as productive of "ragged individualizers," a scattering of thoughtful liberals pointed out during the thirties that, however perverted by selfishness, the ideal of individualism was basically sound. "At the bottom, it asserts that the human individual is all that really counts."[9]

During the depression years, it was difficult for individualists to refute the view that collectivism was inevitable. The growing conviction that individuality was an illusion, or at best an anachronism, and that the world would have to develop collectively, had a kind of mushroom or snowball effect which was to the immense advantage of collectivism. Everywhere the emphasis was on a shared misery, or an enforced equality, which it was hoped would, in time, lead to a new era of plenty. The maldistribution of wealth under competitive capitalism was blamed for the failure of con-

---

[9] T. V. Smith, *The Promise of American Politics* (Chicago: University of Chicago Press, 1936), p. 15.

sumption to keep pace with the productive capacity of modern industry. Economic equality, if it encouraged increased consumption, would be a boon to both reformers and manufacturers.

While the totalitarian state deliberately educated its people to want certain things, in the United States consumer demand was encouraged by advertising and pricing. When the planned and managed economy still failed to produce the desired result of recovery from the depression, the world turned to the artificially induced prosperity of an armaments economy. In the long run this meant war. More immediately, it necessitated economic mobilization with allocation of consumer goods and industrial production. Since armaments were quickly self-destructive, either by use or by obsolescence, full production and employment were achieved in a kind of "bootstrap" operation. The collectivists' assault on individuality was thus based ultimately on the need to go to war. How paradoxical and tragic that the good society or supposed utopia of collectivism, designed to gain a better life for individuals in the mass, should be able to do this only by resorting to war or a war economy! Peoples ready to sacrifice freedom for security seemed also willing to give up life itself.

The conclusion of World War II marked no break in the forces arrayed against individuality. The first of these was militarism, with its implicit respect for authority and its inevitable subordination of the individual personality. In contrast to all previous postwar periods, the end of World War II witnessed no effective demobilization of arms or men. Peacetime conscription is in obvious conflict with the personal freedom of the drafted individual. Secondly, victory over the Axis powers did little to diminish fears of the growth of governmental power or the danger of dictatorship in the world. At the same time, paralleling the expansion of the political state were the ever-increasing economic powers concentrated in the modern corporation.

In the new industrial society, the corporation was almost an entity in itself—the only institution in modern times virtually independent of the state as well as of its own stockholders. Managers and workers alike are largely divorced from their product and, as Peter Drucker has noted, it is the organization, rather than the individual, which is productive.[10] The old idea that the state's functions are political rather than industrial, with the accompanying duty to prevent monopoly, was rendered obsolete as a government–big-business economy succeeded the notion of trustbusting. Finally, and most serious of all for the individual, was the continued sway of nationalism, carried in the decade of the cold war to the extreme of a kind of multilateral nationalism in which the world divided, under American and Russian leadership, into two rival blocs. This new so-called

---

[10] Peter F. Drucker, *The New Society* (New York: Harper, 1950), p. 6.

internationalism was actually a form of interventionism in which competing supernationalisms expanded and projected themselves onto a world scale.

In a world so badly divided, individual insecurity was heightened by the prospect that the atomic weapons of another world war must, in the words of an outstanding scientist, "increase the entropy of this planet, until all distinctions of hot or cold, good and bad, man and matter have vanished in the formation of the white furnace of a new star."[11] With the era of the cold war, national security was in danger of being achieved only at the price of individual freedom. Analyzing the threat inherent in the garrison-police state, Harold Lasswell rephrased Tocqueville to say that "expanded government can be expected to be more centralized government." The centralizing process led to educational and scientific activities becoming more dependent on government, while at the same time the state withheld information, and the press, public opinion, political parties, Congress, courts, and most civilian agencies, all declined in relative if not positive importance.

Contributing effectively to the nationalistic propaganda of cold war was the growing might and power of the mass media. Radio, moving pictures, newspapers and magazines with national circulations, all catered

---

[11] Norbert Wiener, *The Human Use of Human Beings* (Boston: Houghton Mifflin, 1950), p. 142.

to the mass market in which a premium was placed on uniformity of opinion and standardization of taste. While a few writers achieved a numerous clientele, a greater number were left without readers. Even more alarming was the fact that those writers who appealed successfully to a mass market often did so only by satisfying the official or popular view. The mass media, as distinct from the disappearing daily newspaper ruled by a country editor, were thus discouraging to individual artistic and literary achievement.

In the era of postwar prosperity, though there was no lack of personal insecurity or frustration, this uniformity was often condoned by the supposedly consoling argument that the American people had never before enjoyed such material abundance or so high a standard of living. Largely neglected was the antithetical point of view that the people might have to pay for this prosperity "by finding themselves in a centralized and bureaucratized society and world shrunken and agitated by the contact—accelerated by industrialism—of races, nations, and cultures."[12]

From almost any angle of vision or historical perspective, it is difficult to anticipate that the second half of the twentieth century will reverse the long-standing movement toward collectivism and away from individualism. But, at least, the importance of the problem is

---

[12] David Riesman, *The Lonely Crowd* (New Haven: Yale University Press, 1950), p. 18.

being recognized, and in contrast to the former acceptance of the inevitability and desirability of some form of collectivism, a growing body of thought is concerning itself with the preservation of individuality in a free society.

There is perhaps one small, added ray of hope—the encouragement offered by the perversity of the human personality, and the chance that man may still struggle, even against overwhelming odds, to preserve his threatened individual integrity.

Essay Eleven

As a Man Thinketh

Joseph Wood Krutch

Joseph Wood Krutch (1893–1970) was Brander Matthews Professor of Dramatic Literature at Columbia University from 1943 to 1952. In 1954 he received the National Book Award for nonfiction for The Measure of Man; The Desert Year, *published in 1952, won him the John Burroughs Medal.*

A consideration of individuality poses many questions, three of which I should like to examine. They are: (1) Is the term as commonly used meaningful? (2) If so, then is individuality to be regarded as a desirable characteristic? (3) Does the present condition of man promote or discourage it?

The first of these questions has been asked persistently during the past century and the answer implied or stated has very often been in the negative. One cannot be an individual in the traditional sense unless his individuality is a characteristic of some *persona* or *ego* which persists as some sort of unity having a continuous history. All intimate experience conveys the impression that one is such a persisting unity—we feel that "I" has always been "I"—and most Western ethical, religious, and philosophical systems have been based upon the assumption that such a continuous ego is a primary reality.

Of course this assumption was questioned as long ago as the time of Heraclitus, who insisted that flux, not a persistence of identity, was the characteristic of all things including the so-called individual. Upon this was founded the Greek pleasantry about the malefactor who argued that since he was not the man he had been yesterday he could not reasonably be punished for anything he had done then. But it is principally in recent times that the paradox has been widely accepted as simple fact and the doctrine that, for one reason or another, no man is responsible, has been made the basis of legal reforms.

The modern campaign against belief in the individual, the *persona,* or the *ego* as a reality of primary importance has been conducted along at least three fronts.

Something closely related to the Heraclitian paradox has been generally recognized in connection with literature, where what has been called The Dissolution of the Ego is a recognized process. Luigi Pirandello and Marcel Proust come first to mind—Pirandello with his reiterated insistence that no man has a "real character," as distinguished either from the various characteristics which at various times he exhibits or from the idea of that character as different acquaintances formulate it for themselves; Proust with his no less frequently repeated insistence that people change so from day to day that unless one sees them continuously they become quite unrecognizable.

The position taken by Pirandello and Proust (and more or less clearly suggested in much modern literature) goes far beyond the mere recognition that men are often inconsistent. This we all admit. But it does not mean anything to say that a man is inconsistent unless we assume that there is something consistent from which he is temporarily inconsistent. We may say that it is "unlike him" to do this or that. We may solemnly adjure him to "be true to himself" or we may flippantly enjoin him: "Be yourself!" But the recognition of an inconsistency implies a prior and more significant consistency. You cannot be true to yourself unless you have a self. It is just this prior assumption which the dissolvers of the ego deny.

The Christian and the classic conception of the ego seems to have been of a fully conscious unity; of a soul-captain born with us at birth and perhaps created by God. It is an ultimate, even *the* ultimate, reality persisting through time. It may improve itself or it may corrupt itself but it can never cease to *be* itself. Psychology, on the other hand, has eroded this ego away and lent support to its final dissolution as proclaimed in Pirandello and Proust. In the first place, psychology insists that the ego is like an iceberg inasmuch as not more than a fraction is above the surface of the consciousness. In the second place, many psychologists assert that what does occur within the area of consciousness is not direction by an integrated "I" but is the result of a constantly shifting reaction between instinct on the one hand and stimuli and traumas on the other; so that the ego of any moment is simply the temporary result of heredity plus past and present experiences. Individuality becomes, then, no more than the momentary result of the forces which have played upon the so-called individual.

The second front, of the war against the concept of the reality and importance of individuality, here merges with the first. Both Heraclitian flux and the psychology of the unconscious imply that what seems at any moment to be an ego is actually merely an instant in a process. Therefore, since processes are the result of causes, the character of an ego at any moment is the necessary result of external causes operating upon it, never either what it chooses to be or even the inevitable result of what it was in the beginning. It is instead, and like everything else in the universe, inevitably what the forces acting upon it have made it. The will which the ego seems to exercise is, like all the conscious phenomena associated with it, illusory. As Schopenhauer said, we can do what we will but we cannot will what we will will. Everything is determined by something else and we exist in what William James called "a block universe." There are no unmoved movers—which is what the doctrine of free will supposes each *persona* to be.

The man in the street would, perhaps, reject—if he had ever faced—this proposition in its absolute form. Nevertheless he assumes it to be, in general, true.

"Society" is responsible for whatever vices or virtues any man exhibits or, as Paul Lukas, the director of the Society for the Prevention of Crime, has stated very succinctly and absolutely: "In today's thinking, anti-social behavior is considered to be the product of unique economic, sociological, and psychological factors in each offender's past history."

This leaves no room for a captain-of-the-soul or for any responsible ego. Behaviorism as a rigid dogma certainly has fewer adherents than it once did. Nevertheless, it has left so deep a mark upon sociology as well as upon psychology that many, perhaps most, present-day sociologists and psychologists consider human behavior and its determinants the only fruitful subject of study.

The third line of attack follows logically from the other two. The most obvious characteristic of the classical ego is its consciousness. But the significance of consciousness was denied three-quarters of a century ago by Thomas Henry Huxley, who called it merely an "epiphenomenon." The more modern form of this position is expressed in the statement that we do not act because we are conscious but are conscious because we act. The sense of having willed is, for example, simply something which accompanies the choice which external influences have made inevitable.

At any given moment, of course, one man may still differ from another even though he has no continuous personality, is purely the product of forces, and is conscious only because of a shadowy epiphenomenon. To that extent men are still individuals. But I am assuming that in the present consideration individuality of this limited and determined kind is not what we are discussing. I assume further that such individuality as we *are* discussing cannot exist except as an aspect of personality and that the existence of personality implies the existence of some vestige of the classical *ego* surviving the destructive criticism of Heraclitus, Huxley, and J. B. Watson—to take three convenient names.

I suggest further that such an ego can have little significance unless four powers, limited but real, are attributed to it. (1) Such an ego must be conscious and its consciousness must be a primary reality, not an epiphenomenon which is merely a by-product of action. (2) That ego must also be capable of thought, which is to say it must be sometimes capable of reason as distinguished from mere rationalization, which is all that some philosophies grant it. (In other words, Aristotle's statement that man is a reasoning animal must be accepted if it is taken to mean, not an animal who always reasons but an animal who is capable of reasoning.) (3) To some extent, at least, such an ego must be capable also of making a choice not determined by anything outside itself, or in other words must possess some freedom of will; not be exclusively a conditioned machine. (4) Finally, and this is perhaps the most important as well as the most controversial of all, that ego must be capable of making "value judgments" which are not merely the rationalization of the prejudices into which it has been conditioned.

Modern criticism has certainly demonstrated that the ego does not exercise these presumed capacities as frequently as was once assumed. Probably the unconsciousness influences it at least as often as the consciousness. Certainly we often obey our conditioning when we think we are making free choices; often rationalize when we think we are reasoning; and often exhibit prejudices when we think we are making value judgments. But it is hardly demonstrable that we *never* reason, choose, or judge. And there is perhaps no speculative question more important at the present moment than the question whether or not man actually is "nothing but" a conditioned and rationalizing automaton which has somehow or other generated the epiphenomenon called consciousness.

There is, I think, a stronger current of protest against the negative answer to that question, even in the ranks of psychologists, than there was a generation ago. Professor Gordon Allport's "Terry Lectures," published under the title *Becoming,* is a notable discussion which includes some estimate of this trend. On the other hand, some experimenters with "electronic brains" seem convinced that they will ultimately be able to construct a machine exhibiting in at least elementary form all such mental powers as memory, choice, and learning. For these reasons, it seems to me that one of the most fruitful discussions upon which individualists might embark would be just a discussion of the present state of knowledge as it relates to the question whether or not man does give evidence of having a personality in the sense in which I have used the term.

I am not myself capable of giving such an adequate review of the present state of knowledge and opinion. At best, however, the evidence which science can present upon either side falls short of being perfectly conclusive. Therefore, we must act on the assumption that one answer or the other is correct. And this is a case where the answer we do assume has incalculable consequences for society, not only for our attitude toward ourselves, but indeed for the whole experience of living. The question: "Are we men or machines?" is perhaps the most fateful we can ask and one to which we must, in practice, give some answer.

One of America's leading professors of experimental psychology has already proposed that, since man's susceptibility to conditioning has been demonstrated and since his freedom of choice cannot be demonstrated, then education should frankly concern itself, not with the training of either reason or moral judgment, but with the conditioning of its subjects. Surely few questions could be more fateful than this: "Shall we abandon the attempt to train men to think and treat them merely as creatures whose behavior patterns can be set?" Yet that question is only a single illustration of what is at stake.

From what has already been said it is evident that I myself give the pragmatic answer: "We are men." I should, however, like to defend that answer, not by presenting scientific evidence nor by proposing merely the Jamesian formula, but by an argument which rests upon an analogy with certain now generally recognized procedures in a physical science.

Until quite recently most sciences have assumed that a hypothesis is either true or false and that between two contradictory hypotheses the scientist must, at a minimum, adopt one or the other as a working principle. Recently the physicists have frankly rejected this assumption. The ultimate nature of reality, as some have said, is unknown and possibly both unthinkable and unknowable as well. For certain purposes it is necessary to assume one hypothesis, for other purposes another. The classic example of this dilemma is presented by the phenomena associated with light, which must at times be considered an undulation, at other times as a corpuscular stream. Perhaps both hypotheses are, in some way which we cannot conceive, "true."

Now it may possibly be that in some analogous fashion the ego is both free and also what its conditioning has made it. After all, the reconciliation of Fate and Free Will has baffled mankind since the problem was first undertaken. To most people it has seemed impossible to conceive how man could be either free or not free. And the argument between the mechanists and determinists on the one side and the defenders of man as a reasoning, choosing animal on the other, is only one version of this general debate. But too many psychologists and sociologists have, it seems to me, refused to accept the adjustment which so many physicists have now come to.

We have, say many psychologists, evidence that man can be conditioned, no evidence that he can be free. You must either accept our hypothesis that men cannot be free, or you must turn your back, not only upon our evidence, but also upon everything we have learned about how improving the economic condition of a group, for example, may do more than moral suasion to reduce crime. In other words, they are trying to force upon us a choice which the physicist refuses to make. They are saying that a man cannot be in some sense responsible and in some sense not responsible for what he does and is.

Perhaps the time will come when psychology will have demonstrated exactly to what extent and just how an "ego," as I originally defined it, does exist. Perhaps it will some day produce an ethical system and an esthetic system which will reduce both to scientific laws dependent upon the psychology of the human brain. But it has not yet done either and to refuse to discuss ethics or esthetics in any except scientific terms simply compels us to deal very inadequately with both. It does violence also to all our direct experience and dismisses as irrelevant all the intimate experiences of living in favor of an interpretation which even the most convinced must admit does not correspond to his sense of immediate reality.

The most dogmatic determinist and mechanist ponders his problems and makes what even he calls "a decision." If this is not to become a world in which all men are treated as automata, and in which even the individual comes to reject as unreal every intellectual or emotional process in which he finds himself involved, it may be necessary to emulate the boldness of the physicists and say simply: "If I can't reconcile the evidence of psychology and sociology with my own experience, then I will fall back upon paradox. It is sometimes convenient, useful, and even necessary to regard man as a conditioned machine; at other times it is a violation of fundamental human nature not to regard him otherwise."

In this connection it seems illuminating to quote J. Robert Oppenheimer (*Science and the Common Understanding,* Simon and Schuster, 1954):

> It seems rather unlikely that we shall be able to describe in physico-chemical terms the physiological phenomena which accompany conscious thought, or sentiment, or will. . . . [But] should an understanding of the physical correlates of consciousness indeed be available, it will not itself be the appropriate description for the thinking man himself, for the clarification of his thoughts, the resolution of his will, or the delight of his eye and mind at works of beauty.

Speaking specifically of value judgments, or what he calls "the age old problem of good and evil," Professor

Conant (*Modern Science and Modern Man,* Columbia University Press, 1952) said:

> As to the unifying, materialistic World Hypothesis, my doubt stems from its manifest inadequacy. . . . On the other hand, the formulations that attempt to include spiritual values, modern physics, biology and cosmology within one total scheme attempt, to my mind, too much. . . . My preference would be for more adequate exploration of special limited areas of experience; one of these would include those experiences which can be ordered in terms of a system of spiritual values.

To attempt to describe and evaluate individuality entirely in terms of experimentally determinable data is to attempt to foist upon us what Oppenheimer calls "not . . . the appropriate description for the thinking man himself." To try to deal with the moral, esthetic, and intellectual aspects of the individual in similar terms is to reject what Conant calls "more adequate exploration of special limited areas of experience" and his contention that such limited areas of experience must be ordered in terms appropriate to them. It is certainly untrue now (and I believe it always will be untrue) that reason, will, and value judgment can be explored or ordered adequately if we use only terms appropriate to physics, chemistry, sociology, or even experimental psychology.

To take the simplest and mildest possible example, it is, I think, stultifying to attempt (as has so often been done) to substitute for "Virtue" or "Goodness"

some such term as "socially useful." Goodness may be
socially useful but it is also more than merely that,
and the more must not be disregarded. Goodness cannot be an attribute of anything but a *persona;* social
utility may be an attribute of a machine. And here I
would like to add, by way of parenthesis, that the indispensable importance of what are commonly called
humanistic studies and approaches is just that art does
explore the experiences with which it deals in terms
appropriate to them.

So much, then, for the question of whether the term
"individuality," as commonly used, is meaningful. My
second question was: Is individuality as here defined to
be regarded as desirable? My own answer to that question is obviously, Yes.

Perhaps few would answer it definitely No. But it
seems to me obvious that much less value is put upon
individuality now than formerly. It can, I think, hardly
be questioned that educators and sociologists put less
strain than they once did on "the development of individuality" and more on "adjustment"—which may not
be incompatible with individuality but certainly points
in a different direction. Neither can it be questioned
that "normality" has become a key word and that the
tendency is to make little if any distinction between
"normal" and "average," so that the ideal becomes
approximation to a common denominator. Elementary
teachers stress activities and interests "appropriate to
the age group." A society of "normal well-adjusted citi-

zens" seems to mean one in which individuals are as nearly as possible characterized by the same opinions and tastes in intellectual and artistic *as well as* in purely physical matters.

There remains my third question: Does the present condition of man promote or discourage individuality? I must answer that, despite the currently increasing protest against the disparagement of individuality, it is the opinion of many, including myself, that men are tending to become less and less individual. This might well be expected in an atmosphere created by the stress on "normality" and "adjustment" and by the tendency to minimize the importance and even the reality of will, choice, and consciousness. Moreover, many of the specific institutions of our society tend to encourage the growth of conformity. And the influence of society is not denied by even the most passionate defenders of the theory that an individual man is something more than merely the product of social forces.

All forms of mass communication and mass entertainment inevitably tend to submit a larger and larger proportion of the population to precisely the same intellectual and artistic experiences. Large-scale industry and the efficiency of mass production make it more and more profitable to cater exclusively to the lowest common denominator in all things. An increasingly dense population increases the closeness of contact between individuals so that it becomes more and more difficult, physically as well as psychically, to lead any life which does not conform to a prevailing pattern. And since mass industry must cater to mass tastes, advertising uses every possible device to encourage the feeling that one should be ashamed not to want and to get what his neighbor has.

In the arts, stress on the best seller and the Hit Parade tends to create the impression that the most widely accepted art is necessarily the best. Education, instead of countering by emphasizing the excellent rather than the "normal," encourages the general tendency. The large state universities emphasize "preparation for life" rather than "learning" and preparation for life is likely to mean merely vocational training—which is again "adjustment to the existing pattern" in all things. Moreover, the student who enters college has been prepared for this acculturation since kindergarten where "group activity" prevails and, so I have at least been told, the hobbyhorse is sometimes officially frowned upon on the ground that it encourages the young rider to gallop away by himself.

Somewhat less obvious is the fact that the individual worker, either manual or intellectual, is less and less favorably placed by comparison with the member of a team. This is plain enough in the case of "the worker" whose union will be strong in proportion to the number of members who perform the same tasks and have identical interests.

But even the college professor who is a member of

committees making group studies, or engaged in some other cooperative academic enterprise, is the more likely to benefit from subsidies and grants as well as to seem most important to administrators. And perhaps the least obvious but a not unimportant fact is this: Only the worker whose function is essentially that of a robot can enjoy fully the benefits of the increasingly short workweek. No man whose individual personality or talent is essential in his job can function in an organization based upon successive "shifts." Neither the executive, the research scientist, nor, indeed, anyone in any sense creative can drop his work at the end of seven or six hours and have another step into his place. Leisure thus becomes increasingly the special privilege of the robot, and men are encouraged to become robots by the simple fact that "they don't have to work so hard."

Is it any wonder that such an array of forces, ranging all the way from metaphysical convictions to managerial details, should have created the phenomenon called by those who dislike it the Mass Man and by those who approve, "the normal, well-adjusted, common man"?

Whatever we call him, certain of his characteristics are recognized both by his admirers and by his detractors. For instance: He believes that he is living at the most fortunate period of history and looks with pitying contempt upon all the predecessors who were compelled to live in a less "progressive" time. He enthusiastically buys all the newest gadgets, believes that "a high standard of living" is the *summum bonum* and raises a family larger than was common a generation ago.

He attends the most successful movies, buys records of the biggest song hits, and, if he occasionally reads a book, chooses a best seller. His opinions, tastes, and preferences are near those which polls and questionnaires show to be "normal"; and, superficially at least, he seems well content with his lot—whatever some may say of his inner tensions and incipient neuroses. For himself and his family he wants "all the advantages" and believes that he is getting them. That everything from the furniture of his livingroom to the furniture of his mind is nearly indistinguishable from that of everyone he knows, does not disturb him. He believes what the advertisers have told him, namely, that standard brands are best. Any dissatisfaction with any feature of his life which he may begin to feel, and any nonconformity which he may be tempted to indulge, is repressed as a sign of some failure of integration and adjustment.

The lack in such a man is simply this: He has no face. The fact that he not only exists but functions successfully in the struggle for survival is the most convincing argument on the side of those who contend that man is nothing but the product of social forces and that he can be made to accept as right, proper, good, and desirable whatever his society approves. This is the mass man whom the experimental psychologist and the "social engineer" can make. He is also, presumably, the man of the future unless it is true that human nature is something in itself, that man is capable of rebelling and of resisting conditioning. All recent experience indicates that he is more plastic, less capable of choice and of will than was formerly supposed. The undetermined question is whether or not he is *limitlessly plastic and nothing but conditionable.*

Many critics of communism have argued that its fundamental appeal is the release it gives from responsibility and that this release from the necessity of forming opinions, determining actions, or cultivating tastes appeals very strongly to at least the majority of men. Recently Paul Tillich published *The Courage to Be,* a book which propounds the more general thesis that the ego or *persona* is a form of Being in the technical metaphysical sense. If we accept that concept, then the desire to accept a totalitarian authority is simply an obvious outward manifestation of the failure of the "courage to be" and a desire to relapse into that state of nonbeing which is the actual nature of man as mechanistic determinists describe him. One may then say that the mass man is well on the way to becoming the nonman.

In the presence of Samuel Johnson the remark was once made that it is hard to understand why any man should want to make a beast of himself by getting drunk. Johnson replied: "He who makes a beast of himself gets rid of the pain of being a man." So, of course, does he who makes of himself not a beast, but a machine. Communism as a form of government may relieve man of many specific responsibilities. Dialectic materialism as a philosophy relieves him completely of all responsibility to exhibit any "courage to be." Perhaps the sociologist, the anthropologist, and the psychologist who set out to prove that individuality in any meaningful form cannot exist do so because they want to be a machine in order to escape the responsibility (and, as Johnson said, the pain) of being men. Perhaps, then, all the instruments of government, all the institutions of society, and all the methods of education which have been enumerated as tending to encourage the mass man do not actually create him. Perhaps they simply provide many different opportunities and encouragements to escape the responsibilities which consciousness, will, and the power to make value judgments impose upon him.

If this is true, then it is still desirable that those who prefer to *be,* and to be surrounded by others who also *are,* should concern themselves with the governmental, economic, educational, and social forces which provide encouragement to those who prefer nonbeing and thus require of the individual more and more courage if he is to remain an individual, or, in short, to continue to participate in Being. But it is perhaps also true that the most inclusive encouragement of the failure of individuality is simply the scientific and philosophical theory that the characteristics commonly attributed to man as a being are illusory and that, since he cannot in that sense *be,* there is no reason why he should make the attempt or why society should encourage him to do so.

As a man thinketh so he is. Man is tending to become what we have thought that he is.

Collectivism and Individualism

William M. McGovern

William M. McGovern (1897–1964) received doctoral degrees from Oxford, the Sorbonne and the University of Berlin, and was professor of political science at Northwestern University from 1936 until his death in 1964. His interests included anthropology and Oriental studies (he spoke, read and wrote Japanese and Chinese fluently), and he directed expeditions to Tibet, the Amazon basin and Peru, the Near East and Central America. His books include Strategic Intelligence and the Shape of Tomorrow, The War in the Far East *and (with David S. Collier)* Radicals and Conservatives.

The role which the individual can and should play in social, economic, and political life is a problem which has long perplexed both the practical statesman and the abstract philosopher.

In the city states of ancient Greece it was generally thought that the individual should be subordinated to the *polis*. The idea that the private citizen had certain innate or "natural" rights with which the *polis* should not interfere was not so much attacked as ignored. This general attitude was accepted in some form or another by the outstanding political thinkers. Aristotle argued that the chief function of the state was to promote "the good life" among its citizens—by education, if possible; by force, if necessary. The state, moreover, was to be the sole judge of what was and was not "the good life." Plato went even further and theorized that the state, through its rulers or guardians, should regulate in minute detail the moral and economic actions, the literature, the music, and even the thoughts of its citizens.

In the Hellenistic age, and more especially after the rise of Rome to what was considered world supremacy, there was a marked change in attitude. Instead of maintaining that a man lives and moves and has his being solely as a member of a small city state, most persons adopted, without question, the theory which can best be called cosmopolitanism. All men, as men, are members of the human race and this is the one unit that really counts. The Roman Stoics, and the great Roman lawyers, such as Cicero, Gaius, and Ulpian, whom they influenced, applied this conception to the operation of law. According to the Stoics the basis of law is found not in the decrees of any one political unit, but rather in the *jus gentium,* the ideas of just and unjust common to all ethnic groups. *Jus gentium,* in turn, is necessarily based upon *jus naturale,* or natural law, knowable by reason.

This cosmopolitanism prompted an incipient individualism. If men should be governed not by the arbitrary dictates of a city state or a tribal chief, but by general rules, then it becomes incumbent on the individual to understand these rules and apply them to himself. It is more than a coincidence that the later Roman jurisprudence, which developed the theory of cosmopolitanism, also developed the theory of *persona,* or personal and individual rights which the state must carefully respect and protect.

The later Epicurean philosophy, which also exercised great influence upon Rome, was based upon entirely different principles, but it also led to a marked form of individualism. The "highest good" was to be found not in any form of communal life, but rather in each man seeking for himself the type of life which gave him the greatest deep and lasting pleasure.

The barbarian invasions and the collapse of the Roman Empire put an end to abstract discussions regarding the relative merits of collectivism and individualism. When some semblance of order was restored, during the latter part of the Middle Ages, there developed a very peculiar and interesting situation, a sort of compromise between collectivism and individualism. Extreme individualism was rejected. No one claimed that each man had the right to think, to speak, and to act as he pleased. It was generally agreed that the individual was of importance only through being a member of some group. At the same time, extreme collectivism was rejected because the ordinary man was a member of and subject to the rules of one or more different, competitive groups, no one of which could secure complete power over the populace.

Extreme collectivism in the form of statism, the complete subjection of the citizen to the state, was rendered impossible by the fact that the power of such states as existed was sharply limited by two types of forces, one of these international or supernational, the other intranational or subnational. By far the most important of the supernational forces was the Catholic church, under the leadership of the Pope. It was universally believed that the church had jurisdiction over all Christians, irrespective of the particular country in which they dwelt, or of the particular temporal ruler to whom they owed allegiance. This, in turn, meant that the particular states were prohibited from passing laws which might be contrary to the doctrines of the supernational church. Thus the particular states could not enact laws regarding marriage and divorce or laws regarding testaments, as all such matters were held to be under ecclesiastical jurisdiction.

The state was thus strictly limited in its powers and its functions by supernational forces. It was also subject to important limitation by forces within the state. Medieval Europe was strongly influenced by feudalism, and by feudal law most of the nobles were held to have certain inherent rights and privileges with which the state could not lawfully interfere. The relations between the ruler and his vassal lords were not subject to general legislation; such matters were regulated by private contract or agreement between the two parties. The duties which one vassal owed to his lord, and the tribute which he should pay, differed widely from the duties and financial obligations of other vassals.

In like manner it became customary to grant special charters to various cities and towns and to the various guilds and corporations within these municipalities. These charters bestowed special rights and privileges upon the municipalities or corporations concerned. Since the rights and privileges varied from case to case, it was extremely difficult to pass general legislation affecting all these subordinate bodies. Normally, these charters could not be revoked or seriously amended without the consent of all the parties concerned. This meant a practical limitation on the authority of central government in the interest of autonomous groups and therefore to some extent in the interest of the individuals composing them.

In the later Middle Ages the rulers of the secular states were also limited by the development of legislative assemblies, variously called *Cortes, Etâts Generaux, Parliaments,* etc. These were chosen, in one way or another, by the spiritual and temporal nobility, by the landowning gentry, and by the leading guilds of the various municipalities. This development was of importance not merely as a means of curbing the ambitions of the monarch but also by introducing the idea that group interests must be considered in any attempt to increase the power of the state as a whole over its subjects.

The forces which led to the Renaissance and the Reformation swept away the social, economic, and political conditions which had prevailed in most of Western Europe during the Middle Ages. The medieval compromise of pluralism ceased to influence most Europeans, and the fundamental struggle between collectivism and individualism again came to the fore.

At first the forces favoring collectivism were strikingly successful. During the first part of the sixteenth century the secular rulers of most states enormously increased their powers. As these secular rulers came to be more and more identified with the state itself, this meant that both the power and the influence of the state were also greatly amplified.

Part of this transformation was the direct result of the Reformation. This nationalistic rising gave a staggering blow to the papacy and to the supernational ecclesiastical hierarchy which the Pope headed. In the countries which accepted Protestantism the papal court no longer had any substantial jurisdiction. Canon law was rejected and ecclesiastical courts were abolished. The secular ruler successfully claimed complete control over all persons within his domain, irrespective of whether they were or were not in holy orders. Much of the vast material wealth of the church was confiscated; that which remained was subject to secular taxation.

The new Protestant churches, moreover, were in most cases completely subordinated to the secular authority. In England, Henry VIII was formally proclaimed Supreme Head of the Anglican church. It was the king who now decided what the organization, the ritual, and the articles of faith were to be. In the countries which adopted Lutheranism the situation was not very different. Luther, to be sure, insisted that the true church was the church invisible, consisting of all sanctified persons, whether living or dead. But he also emphasized the need for a visible church, consisting of flesh and blood members, whether sanctified or not, and he was perfectly willing to see this visible church controlled by the secular authorities. As a result, in most Lutheran countries the established church became in effect a special branch of the temporal government.

Even in the countries which as a whole retained spiritual allegiance to Rome, the papacy lost much of its erstwhile power over the secular rulers. The kings of France, for example, remained Roman Catholics, but nevertheless demanded almost as much freedom from ecclesiastical control as those monarchs who had gone over to Protestantism. By virtue of a special concordat with the Pope, King Francis I secured the right to nominate all members of the French ecclesiastical hierarchy. Moreover, it was agreed that no papal bulls could be promulgated in France without the consent of the French monarch.

As the Reformation was undermining the supernational religious check upon the new nation-states, there developed a coincident movement which led to the weakening of those internal forces which had likewise curbed the authority of central government. With the rise of commerce feudalism decayed and during the sixteenth century the kings of the various countries were able to check, and even abolish, many of the special privileges and rights which had been held by the great feudal nobility.

At the same time, the power and the influence of the chartered municipalities and corporations tended to dwindle. This is somewhat surprising as this period witnessed an enormous growth of trade and industry, which in turn brought about a great increase of the urban middle class. But that growth itself weakened the restrictions imposed by the medieval charters. Above all, the merchants needed law and order, and it seemed to them that this could best be secured by strengthening the authority of central government.

Centralized national authority was also aided by the attrition of the embryonic parliamentary institutions established under feudalism. These had made consent of the legislative assembly necessary for the levying of taxes upon landed property, leaving the monarchs free to gather other taxes as they saw fit. In most countries the royal governments levied internal and external customs dues at will. With the growth of trade and industry these taxes brought in an ever-larger revenue, with the result that the rulers were no longer so dependent upon legislative grants. The kings of Spain and Portugal grew enormously wealthy from the tribute paid to them personally from the newly founded colonies in America and in Asia. So it is not surprising that the legislative assemblies which had formerly been so important began to lose their influence. The *Cortes* of Spain and Portugal, and the corresponding bodies in France and the Germanic countries were convened less and less frequently and eventually faded out. In England, Parliament continued to assemble, but under the Tudor monarchs it became completely subservient to the royal commands.

Unquestionably this slow but steady growth of centralized government met with general approbation. Far from looking with dread at the increasing powers of the central government, the general populace welcomed the decay of the oppressive feudal nobility and of the monopolistic corporations. This sentiment was strengthened by the printing press and growing urban literacy. Writers such as Belloy, Barclay, and Filmer defended the "divine right" of an absolute ruler in an all-powerful state. Today such men are largely forgotten, but in their own time they enjoyed immense popularity. Of more lasting influence were the writings of Jean Bodin, the great French thinker, who glorified the powerful centralized state from a more philosophical point of view. Most important of all were the doctrines put forth by that outstanding English political philosopher, Thomas Hobbes.

The basic part of Hobbes' political thought was centered around the theory of *sovereignty,* an idea first enunciated by Bodin but greatly expanded and clarified in the Hobbesian philosophy. The theory of sovereignty falls into two parts. First is the declaration that within every state at any given moment a person or a group of persons in fact possesses absolute power. Hobbes used this phase of the theory to argue in favor of frankly delegating all the powers of the state to an absolute monarch. More significant today is the second part of the theory: that the state ought to possess sole ultimate power over all persons and groups of persons within its territory. This eliminates any possibility of the state being curbed by a supernational agency, such as the church, or by any corporation or other vested interest within the state. It asserts that no individual has any right, natural or other, to disobey or disregard the dictates of political government.

According to Hobbes, the state has not only the right but also the duty to suppress any opinion or expression of opinion deemed by the ruler contrary to the security of the state. "The actions of men proceed from their opinion and in the well governing of opinion consisteth the well governing of man." It is the duty of the state to lay down not merely what is legal and illegal, but also what is moral and immoral. "All subjects are bound to obey that for divine law which is declared to be so by the laws of the commonwealth."

In the economic sphere, moreover, Hobbes argues that the state has complete jurisdiction over the property of its citizens. To Hobbes' totalitarian thought, all property rights within a state are only the result of the grant of such rights by the state, and what the state gives, it can also take away.

The collectivism of Hobbes is an obvious precursor of modern totalitarianism. But even as Hobbes was writing, a new movement was taking form which put renewed emphasis upon individualism. This had its origins among religious groups which felt that they were being persecuted by the temporal authorities. Interestingly enough, it was the early Jesuits and the early Calvinists who unconsciously and unwittingly laid the foundations for the new individualism. Neither the Jesuits nor the Calvinists were concerned with individual liberty as such, but rather with defending the interest of their respective churches. To this end both groups were agreed that the state was a purely human organization and should be subordinated to the church, a divine organization.

In this way both the Jesuits and the Calvinists denied that the secular state should have complete and absolute control over its subjects. As long as the state was subordinate to and controlled by the church, people should obey the temporal laws without complaint. But suppose that the laws of the state were contrary to the laws of the church, and that the state actually persecuted the church? In that event men should obey God (represented by the church) rather than the king, and in case of persecution the people had both the right and the duty to rise in rebellion, if the church so ordered. Having gone thus far, both the Jesuits and the Calvinists went even further, affirming that the people have the right to rebel against a tyrannical ruler, even when the grounds of dispute are not theological.

By historical accident, it was the Calvinists who took the lead in developing the doctrine of the right of subjects to rebel against secular authority, a doctrine which later led to the revival of individualism. While Calvin himself was supreme in Geneva, many of his followers in other lands were subject to persecution by the secular authorities, which tended to make them inimical to the whole theory of the completely sovereign state. In France, in the Netherlands, and in Scotland, the Calvinists broke into open rebellion more than once.

Of even greater importance, historically, is the fact that Calvinism had a strong influence upon the English Puritans and hence upon the Puritan revolution against Charles I. At first the orthodox Puritans were not concerned with individualism. They merely wished to get rid of the bishops, curb the king, and Calvinize the national church. But Cromwell and many of his fellow soldiers went beyond orthodox Calvinism in their views regarding the church. Instead of a national church, they wanted a free association of local churches and claimed that within limits each church should be allowed to formulate its own doctrines. This helped to popularize the belief that it was a duty to rebel against any government which attempted to interfere with ideas, or with actions based upon the individual's conscientious sense of what was right or wrong. This doctrine received its most eloquent expression in the *Areopagitica* of John Milton, at one time Cromwell's Latin secretary. In this essay Milton argued convincingly not only for freedom of thought and expression, but also for freedom of moral action—the right of each man to do as he pleases so long as he does not injure his neighbors.

The revolutionary government of the Puritan Commonwealth was not popular. After Cromwell's death it rapidly disintegrated, and the Stuarts were restored to the English throne. The works of Milton were burned by the public hangman. For a while it seemed as if absolutism would be triumphant. But less than thirty years later (in 1688) the arbitrary actions of James II brought on a new revolution. Thereafter England was to be ruled by a strictly limited monarchy. There was also a great revival of individualism, both in theory and in practice.

Just at this time John Locke brought out his little work on *Civil Government* in which was incorporated a well-reasoned and stirring plea for individualism. The ideas expounded in this book had a profound influence upon Western Europe and the American colonies. They were, as Thomas Jefferson freely admitted, incorporated by him into the American Declaration of Independence (1776), which might almost be called a *Reader's Digest* version of Locke's work.

The basis of Locke's philosophy is the supremacy of Reason. To his way of thinking, Reason (with a capital R) can give us a solution to all human problems, moral, social, and political. He assumes that men are essentially rational and hence can be trained to use their reason in the conduct of their affairs. Man must also be considered to be essentially good. Unless corrupted by passions and prejudices, men tend to do what reason tells them is good and avoid what reason tells them is bad. Finally, men must be considered more or less equal. They are not, of course, absolutely equal in their capacities and attainments, but the differences between them are relatively unimportant and are largely the result of differences in environment and upbringing.

According to Locke, men originally lived in an isolated, prepolitical state of nature. In this condition everyone possessed a set of natural rights (life, liberty, and property) and was governed only by a set of rational principles called natural law. Because of the inconvenience of primitive society men eventually came together and, by means of a formal social contract, created the political unit known as the state. To this state was granted certain limited, but very limited, powers. These powers were limited because, when men agreed to create the state, they retained most of their natural rights, and with these retained or reserved rights the artificial state should never, under any circumstances, interfere. In fact, the only true function of the state is to repel foreign invaders and to punish domestic crime. As long as a man refrains from injuring his neighbors (thereby committing a crime), he has an absolute right to think, to say, and to do what he pleases. It is no function of the state to make its citizens either wise or good. Nor is it the state's function to make them prosperous, as the general prosperity can best be secured by permitting complete *laissez faire* in economic affairs.

At the end of the eighteenth century Jeremy Bentham promulgated his utilitarian philosophy, which attracted a large following, especially in England. This philosophy differed from Locke's system in several important respects, but it was equally fervent in defending an individualism which today would seem extreme to many. Bentham agreed with Locke in stressing the supremacy of reason. Bentham also agreed that all men are basically rational, at least to the extent that they are capable of judging what things and what measures will best promote their own advantage. They are not only basically equal, they are also basically homogeneous, so that irrespective of time or place they are motivated by the same emotions and desires. Bentham refused to admit that men are basically good in the sense that they are motivated by moral principles. He claimed that man's sole motivation is rational self-interest. But he insisted that in a properly organized society each man, by a sort of natural harmony, when working for his own interest automatically helps to advance the interest of his fellow citizens.

Bentham rejected Locke's ideas regarding the pre-political state of nature and the social contract. He was not concerned with conditions in primitive times, nor with the problems of how states originated. He was only interested in how states *should* function and how governments *should* act. In seeking an answer to this problem, he rejected Locke's theories of natural law and natural rights and all other conventional ideas of moral obligation. He was convinced that pleasure is the only good, and pain the only evil. From the point of view of the individual everything and every law is good which increases his pleasure and everything is bad which increases his pain. From the point of view of society and the state, institutions and laws are good when they promote the greatest happiness (or pleasure) for the greatest number of the populace. And institutions or laws are bad when they increase the happiness of only a few at the expense of many.

It was on the basis of the "greatest happiness" principle that Bentham defended individualism. The vast majority of people are rendered unhappy when the state interferes with what they think or say or write; hence the need for freedom of thought and expression. Bentham was bitterly opposed to any attempt by the state to impose morality by legal action. In the first place it is ineffective; morality cannot be enforced. Even more important, any attempt to enforce it will result in widespread unhappiness and hence is evil. Punishment should be confined to actions in which one person injures another. In like manner, people are rendered unhappy when the state interferes with their economic activity. A man is rendered unhappy when the state tells him what he can and cannot plant or manufacture, or what kind of a job he should take. For this reason the "greatest happiness" principle demands a rigorous "let alone," or *laissez faire,* policy.

Until the middle of the nineteenth century individualism remained the prevailing creed of nearly all the

English-speaking peoples. About 1870, however, a new type of collectivism arose which rapidly became popular and was able to dominate a large section of public opinion in the first half of the twentieth century, first in England and later in the United States.

There were many different forces and political ideologies which produced and augmented the desire for collectivism during this period. The first important steps towards collectivism were taken by men who ignored abstract theorizing and who were motivated either by humanitarianism or by political expediency. Humanitarianism was a strong factor in the adoption of many legislative measures which called for the regulation of commerce and industry by the state. For this reason it is not surprising that these measures were initiated by men who were far from being radical collectivists; many were aristocrats who felt that society has a moral duty to protect the poor, the weak, and the unfortunate. Thus some of the earlier English "Factory Acts," which limited the employment of women and children and regulated the conditions under which even men might labor, were sponsored by the Earl of Shaftesbury, a staunch Tory who regarded socialism as the child of the devil.

Later, after the rise of organized labor to a position of political power, humanitarianism was largely replaced by political expediency as the main force leading towards collectivism. This was no new phenomenon. In ancient Rome demagogues were in the habit of securing and maintaining power by the offer of *panem et circenses* (bread and circuses) to the mob. But there this dispensation of *largesse* was largely confined to the inhabitants of the capital city. Under the modern state the distribution is much more widespread. Practical politicians seldom theorize about the merits or demerits of collectivism in the abstract, but such persons are anxious to be elected or returned to office and find it expedient to promise special favors to large organized groups. Sometimes these favors take the form of money subsidies (veterans' bonus, etc.). More frequently the favors take the form of special rights and privileges granted to large blocs of voters. In addition to curbing free economic activity, some parts of this program soon tend to contradict others. Thus many laws have been passed favoring tenants at the expense of landlords (rent control); employees at the expense of employers (minimum wage); producers at the expense of consumers (price support); and consumers at the expense of producers (price control).

For the past century, however, there has been no lack of writers who defend collectivism on abstract or theoretical grounds. Some of these may be called neo-utilitarians, for they accept many of Bentham's premises, though differing radically as regards the conclusions to be drawn from these premises. Bentham himself thought that the greatest happiness of the greatest number (the ultimate aim of the state) would be promoted by strict individualism. But he was careful to deny that the individual or the minority has any "natural" or "inalienable" right which may not be interfered with on moral grounds. On Bentham's own principles, if at any time it could be shown that individualism promotes unhappiness and that socialism or even communism promotes happiness on the part of the majority, then it would follow that individualism is morally wrong and that socialism or communism is morally right. It is the essence of neo-utilitarianism to claim that individualism does lead to poverty and misery on the part of the "masses" (the majority) and that collectivism should therefore be the goal of the political reformer.

The latter part of the nineteenth century also witnessed the rise of another school of English political thought, differing from that of neo-utilitarianism on many basic points but equally favorable to collectivism. This was the idealist school, originating among a group of Oxford scholars (T. H. Green, B. Bosanquet, etc.) but very strongly influenced by the teachings of Hegel —so much so that the members of this group are frequently called neo-Hegelians. Hegel, himself, was strongly influenced by certain phases of Rousseau's philosophy, especially by his theory of the general will.

The English idealists, like the Franco-Swiss Rousseau before them, made a sharp distinction between the ephemeral desires, wishes, and caprices of a man and his allegedly true *will,* which is his "free moral will." Man's desires frequently lead him astray and make him commit evil acts. His will, however, is always basically good, as it constantly seeks to promote the true well-being of each man and as true well-being is only to be found in the "good" or the "worthwhile" life. True freedom, therefore, is to be found not in following one's animal desires or caprices, but in doing what the rational will tells us we ought to do. Liberty does not mean "doing what one likes." It is rather "a positive power of doing and enjoying something worth doing and enjoying."

From these premises the idealists proceeded to draw strong collectivist conclusions. Because of certain external conditions, they argued, it is frequently impossible for the "free moral will" to function. In such cases it is the duty of the state to remove these hindrances or obstacles to freedom. To Green, a man dominated by a passion for drink is not free, but a slave of alcohol. Hence, when the state curbs or prohibits the liquor traffic, it is actually removing an obstacle to freedom. Green held similar views regarding other "social evils" of his day. Thus he was convinced that the state should prohibit all gambling, as an obstacle to the operation of the free moral will. In like manner, not only should the state abolish organized prostitution; it should also seek to eliminate all extramarital sex relations, on the grounds that if the state tolerates uninhibited passion it is failing to remove a roadblock on the path toward true freedom.

When Green came to deal with economic matters, it

is not surprising to find him arguing that true freedom, as he defines it, necessitates a great deal of governmental regulation and control. In all economic matters "the mere enabling of a man to do as he likes is in itself no contribution to freedom." According to Green, men are not truly free if they are overworked and if their wages are inadequate for the essential needs of livelihood. Consequently, Green was in favor of regulating by law both the hours and the compensation of industrial workers.

In the light of subsequent developments, Green's concrete proposals for collectivist legislation now seem comparatively mild. It must be noted, however, that many of the later idealists became ardent advocates of Fabian socialism on the ground that Green's vision of "true freedom" could only be fulfilled by a system involving the complete nationalization of all commerce and industry.

Even the more radical of the English idealists were moderate compared with some of the Continental followers of the Hegelian school of thought. It is generally agreed that the collectivism of Bismarckian Germany was a concrete embodiment of many Hegelian ideals. Of even greater importance is the influence of the extreme, though bitterly hostile, wings of the Hegelian movement.

Its extreme right wing led to the development of the ideology underlying national socialism (Nazism), fascism, and other similar movements. In these systems there are also many non-Hegelian elements. But the writings of Hitler and Mussolini show that most of the basic doctrines of national socialism and fascism are essentially logical developments of certain basic Hegelian ideas.

Of great influence was Hegel's belief that the state is the highest manifestation of the Divine Spirit in space and time, that "the state is the march of God in the world." Associated with this doctrine was the ideal that the dictates of the state are higher and more important than the dictates of any abstract system of morality or "natural" law. This in turn led to the doctrine that the true (as opposed to the apparent) will of each man is identical with the "general will" of the state, and that a man is truly free only if he unreservedly accepts the dictates of the state—the concrete embodiment of the general will.

The extreme left wing of the Hegelian movement is typified by the doctrines of Karl Marx. There are, of course, many features of Marxism which are of non-Hegelian origin, but the solid core of this system, with its reliance on dialectic and its insistence on the allegedly inevitable trend toward collectivism, is rooted in Hegelian ideology, as Marx was the first to admit. Rousseau's and Hegel's theory of "true" freedom also led to the defense of absolute dictatorship by the Communist Party leaders. If a man is really free, he does only what his "true" will demands that he do; and it follows that men are free only when they obey the dictates of those who express a popular will which is true because it is general, and general because it is true.

Even today practically all of the Social Democratic or Socialist parties of continental Europe claim to be inspired by Marx, though they now tend to preach a rather watered-down version of the Marxist creed. The orthodox or "fundamentalist" followers of Marx are, of course, the Russian and Chinese Communists and their adherents in other parts of the world.

At the close of World War II it appeared to many that collectivism in one or other of its modern aspects was bound to engulf the world, and it is still possible that this will be the outcome. The military collapse of Germany, Italy, and Japan did little to stem the tide, as this only meant that the threat of the extreme right-wing collectivism of Hitler and his allies was replaced by the even more serious threat of extreme left-wing collectivism embodied in the Communist movement.

Currently, however, there appears to be a turning of the tide, which may prove of major historical significance. For the time being, at least, the threat of the expansion of communism by force of arms has been checked. Of even greater importance is the fact that there are now rumblings behind the iron curtain. It is probable that the Soviet armed forces can suppress any open rebellion, unless the Free World is willing to supply military aid; but it is clear that there is widespread dissatisfaction with the operation of the Communist regime. Outside the iron curtain there was at one time widespread sympathy with Communist goals, even among non-Communists. Much of this sympathy has now disappeared. Even among the Fabian socialists there is a great deal of disillusionment about the results of the nationalization of industry, as can be seen in the *New Fabian Essays* published in England, and in such a work as *Democratic Socialism—A Reappraisal,* by Norman Thomas, for many years the leader of the American socialist movement.

It would appear that the time is now ripe for the creation and development of a new school of individualism. If such a school is to thrive and prove of real importance, however, it must be founded upon a type of individualism which is both sane and moderate. It must also be based upon a sounder knowledge of human nature and of human history than was characteristic of some of the earlier schools of individualism.

The older individualism was based upon the theory that men are equal, that they are rational, and that they are good. The new individualism must admit that men are far from being equal (even though it recognizes that they should be equal before the law). It must recognize that, though men are capable of the use of reason, many human actions are motivated by nonrational and even downright irrational impulses. It must realize that the idea of "original sin," or at least of human frailty and sinfulness, is more than idle theology; that man while in a barbarous state needed the strict discipline of customary law to make him into a decent being; and that even today when men are weaned away from all traditional moral codes they are apt to revert to animal cruelty.

The new individualism must realize that in the so-called prepolitical state men did not live in isolation. In fact, in very early times men lived in close-knit kinship groups, and apparently the individual was completely subordinated to the group as a whole. What he ate, what he wore, what he did, what he said, what he thought were all the result of customary law imposed by the group. Collectivism, not individualism, characterized man's primitive condition.

Individualism is something which men have developed through centuries of cultural progress. Individualism is possible only among people who are culturally mature. Modern collectivism is merely an artificial regression to barbaric practice. In contrast to Fabian socialism, which seeks to secure the advance of socialism slowly and gradually, the new individualists should seek to be Fabian individualists, striving to secure an individualistic philosophy slowly and gradually, and only to the extent that men prove worthy of exercising their individual rights.

The old individualism was apt to reject all reference to tradition, to the accumulated experience and wisdom of the ages, arguing that individual reason was a sufficient guide for the conduct of life. The new individualism must realize that, though men should not be slaves to tradition, they would do well to be aware of, and to profit by, what the experience of former generations has shown to be the best means of pursuing "the good life." We shall improve upon our ancestors not by ignoring them, but rather by building further upon the foundations they laid down.

Our ultimate goal must be the complete freedom of the individual in thought, in expression of thought, and in action, but we must realize that in the present imperfect world it is sometimes necessary to restrict a lesser freedom in order to secure and preserve a greater freedom. In order to preserve a free society it is sometimes necessary to place restrictions upon persons engaged in an organized conspiracy to abolish all freedom in favor of totalitarianism.

We must hold freedom of speech as something sacred, but it is sometimes necessary to prohibit a man from shouting "fire" in a crowded theater. We must carefully avoid all attempts to impose morality by state action. A man is truly moral only when he freely chooses virtue in spite of his ability to choose vice. Nevertheless, we may well act collectively to prohibit the white slave traffic, the narcotics traffic, or organized juvenile delinquency.

We cannot have true freedom when individual initiative in the economic sphere is prohibited, and when the all-powerful state owns and operates all or most of the means of production and distribution. Individual freedom is impossible in the absence of private enterprise. At the same time society must step in to prevent fraud or the rise of monopoly. It must also step in when any group, whether management or labor, takes advantage of its power and seeks to exploit the other sections of society.

Above all, we must reverence the dignity and worth of the individual. We should fully realize that this conception is wholly derived from spiritual and moral values. This, in turn, means that the new individualism, if it is to rise and prosper, can never reject or even ignore those higher values.

Index

This book was linotype set in the Times Roman series of type. The face was designed to be used in the news columns of the *London Times*. The *Times* was seeking a type face that would be condensed enough to accommodate a substantial number of words per column without sacrificing readability and still have an attractive, contemporary appearance. This design was an immediate success. It is used in many periodicals throughout the world and is one of the most popular text faces presently in use for book work.

Book design by Design Center, Inc., Indianapolis, Indiana
Typography by Weimer Typesetting Co., Inc., Indianapolis, Indiana
Printed and bound by Edwards Brothers, Inc., Ann Arbor, Michigan